This book is dedicated to a spirit of a free press whose purpose is to inform the public through pictures and words—photojournalism.

Ron Galella

ACKNOWLEDGMENTS

I wish to acknowledge with gratitude my lawyers, the first to represent a paparazzo and his rights as a photojournalist.

Alfred S. Julien

Stuart A. Schlesinger

David Jaroslawicz

Bennett D. Brown

I am particularly grateful to Lee H. Smith who not only read my manuscript but edited it and made invaluable suggestions.

I would also like to extend my deepest appreciation to the photographers who have permitted me to reproduce photographs taken of me in this book. They are:

Joy Smith, pages 45, 46

Vito D'Erasmo, page 70

Alpha Blair, page 73

Tom Wargacki, page 59, 72

Donna Graham, page 75

Marvin Koner, page 75

Peter Gould, page 151

Ann Phillips, page 172

Paul Schmulbach, page 176

Sasa Wargacki, page 200

contents

Introduction: THE FOCUS

First of all, what is a paparazzo? When I looked the word up in an Italian dictionary, I couldn't find it. Webster's dictionary defines it as a 'freelance photographer.' Since that hardly satisfied my curiosity, I wrote a letter to the famed Italian movie director Federico Fellini, who first coined the expression in his great 1960 film *La Dolce Vita*. Fellini gave the name "Signor Paparazzo" to one of the photographers in the movie who scurried up and down Rome's Via Veneto taking pictures of movie stars and other celebrities.

"When I was a schoolboy in Rimini," Fellini explains, "I shared a desk with a very restless boy who was always squirming, who was always talking so fast that his words came out stuck together in an endless buzzing. A teacher baptized him "Paparazzo," which in my part of the country is an insect, a sort of mosquito that's always emitting a buzz. While I was writing the script for *La Dolce Vita* that nickname came to mind, and so I named one of the photo-reporters Paparazzo."

The name stuck, not only in Rome, but everywhere. Now all those freelance, freebooting, freeloading photographers who lurk in the shadows of those otherwise glittering capitals of the fashionable world—New York, Paris, London, St. Tropez, Rome, Acapulco, Capri,—are called paparazzi.

This book was written out of an honest conviction to communicate, through words and pictures, my viewpoint, my philosophy, and my style as a freelance photographer. It is my answer as to why and how I specialize in photographing celebrities in this manner.

"Photography with the PAPARAZZI approach" is the slogan I use on my letterhead and business cards, and my logo lists the qualities that I try to evoke in my pictures, that is, that they be off-guard, unrehearsed, spontaneous in expression and gesture. I don't make appointments, of course; even if the celebrities I photograph could afford the time, the results would be lacklustre because my subject would be performing for the camera. The candid picture of an unaware subject has greater meaning and value because it communicates the flavor of life—something that studio photography can't approach.

I call my technique "the only game." Superstars like Jackie Onassis, Elizabeth Taylor or Elvis Presley hire press agents and bodyguards so that they only have to deal with the press and the public on their own terms. Famous personalities use their press agents not to keep the public informed, but to keep themselves in the best possible light—a light which may not shine on real life. I believe that photographers like myself are artists and therefore have the right to have control over their medium. Thus, "the only game" becomes the job of breaking through this wall of press agents and bodyguards to get to the stars directly, tracking them down and photographing them in airports, streets, theatres and hotel lobbies. To succeed, a paparazzo may break academic rules, but he doesn't need to break the law.

Can paparazzi photojournalism be justified? Two fundamental opposing rights are involved: the individual's right to privacy and the public's right to be informed. This book offers my own point of view. I offer it in the hope that the paparazzi approach will be accepted in America as it already has in most of the world.

1

what makes Jackie run?

It was a warm and hazy afternoon in the early fall. I remember that. It was Monday, October 4th, 1971, and it was the start of the best week I ever had, the most successful week I ever had photographing Jackie. The light was so nice and soft that afternoon that I could just set my black and white at f/8-1/250 of a second and not worry too much.

I hadn't seen Jackie in over five months. She had been away with Ari in Europe, on Skorpios mostly. I didn't follow them to Skorpios that summer. I had enough of Skorpios from the year before. I don't ever want to go back to Skorpios again. I might get killed. Besides, I had other plans for the summer of 1971. I went to Mexico, to Cuernavaca, to photograph Elizabeth Taylor and Richard Burton filming *Hammersmith Is Out.* That's where security men caught me hiding in a cave near the set and beat me up. But that's another story.

I knew that Jackie had come back to New York because I knew she always came back to bring the children to their private schools–Caroline to Brearley and John to Collegiate Boys School. Jackie is good that way. I think that she is a very good mother.

Jackie's apartment is on Fifth Avenue and 85th Street, across from Central Park. From the outside the building doesn't look like anything too special, but it is nice with its green canopy and a doorman in a dark blue uniform with white gloves and a silver whistle for calling cabs. It is a good neighborhood, but I think that New York is too dangerous these days, too much crime. That's why I moved out to Yonkers. I don't want anybody busting into my place when I'm off to Europe or Mexico. Of course with a doorman and everything Jackie doesn't have to worry as much about protection as I do. Jackie paid $200,000 for her co-op apartment and it has 15 rooms. Or so I understand. She has never invited me inside.

And so I stopped by a little after 4 o'clock that afternoon to make a spot-check, to find out where Jackie was and what she was up to. The best way to find out where Jackie is would be to ask the doorman of her building. He knows. But he won't tell me because he's on her side. And I don't blame him. If he started giving me information, he could get fired. And so what I do is ask the doorman of the building next door. He won't lose his job, but he is not completely safe either. You know what the Secret Service can do to him? They can park their cars right in front of his building. That way he can't save any parking places for his tenants, and he loses his tips. So even the doorman next door has to be careful. To make him a little braver I give him $10.00 whenever he gives me a good lead, whenever his information results in some pictures.

On this particular day he told me that Jackie had gone across the street to the park with Caroline just a little while ago. "How were they dressed?" I asked him. "Were they carrying anything?" You have to play detective. You have to know what to be prepared for. "Yes," he told me, "They were carrying tennis rackets."

That was good news. Half a year ago I received a letter from the editor and publisher of *Tennis* magazine asking me if I had any pictures of Jackie playing or even watching tennis. There are always special requests like that. *Women's Wear Daily* had a standing request for a picture of Jackie in hot pants. She has three pairs but no photographer has ever caught her wearing them. I didn't have any pictures of Jackie

The day of the famous running scene, a neighboring doorman told me that Jackie and Caroline had headed for the park with tennis rackets.

14   A woman gave me that "get lost" look—and then I saw
     Jackie right in front of me!

on the tennis court either and here was a good chance to fill that request.

The park was beautiful that day with the kids riding bicycles and the nannies wheeling baby carriages. I walked to the reservoir, which is like a big clean lake in the middle of Central Park with a fence around it. It's very clean. I like that. When I finally got to the tennis courts I asked an older woman sitting on a bench, "Have you seen Jackie?"

She looked at my cameras. She looked at me. I knew from experience that this one wouldn't tell me anything. She was on Jackie's side and she gave me a "get lost" look. A lot of people are like that and this woman was the type who would stick her hand into your lens and say, "Leave her alone." Old women in particular are like that. During my trial I used to get phone calls at home. Once, I got a phone call at three in the morning and this old woman's voice said:

"Leave Jackie alone."

"Who is this?" I asked.

"Leave Jackie alone."

Then she hung up. It was spooky. But that's part of being a paparazzo.

It didn't matter that the woman on the bench didn't tell me anything because just then I saw Jackie herself only about ten feet away from me. She looked good. Healthy. Natural. I was happy to see that. Jackie may think I like to catch her looking bad, that I want to embarrass her. But that's not true. I want to make her look good, but spontaneous, natural, the way she really is. Not posed. I like to see her looking good. The pictures sell better that way, too.

I like Jackie. She doesn't understand that. It's more than liking her, I don't know what you'd call it, but I know that I'd be almost nothing today without her. She thinks that I just want to humiliate her but that is not true. I couldn't have followed her for all those years and taken all those pictures of her, thousands of pictures of her—if I didn't feel something for her. She is my ideal subject.

I don't take ugly pictures of Jackie. If I have an unattractive picture of Jackie I tear it up. She's too beautiful to permit the camera to play tricks on her, as it sometimes can do to anyone, no matter how attractive they are. Anyway, ugliness isn't what all the women in the drugstores and the supermarkets with their copies of *Modern Screen* and *Cosmopolitan* want to see. They are tired of war and ugliness and poverty and conflict. They want to see glamour, beauty, wealth and success stories about famous people. They want to see Jackie at the tennis court on a lovely fall afternoon in Central Park. And they want to see her as being even more beautiful than she really is.

I don't know if Jackie saw me right away or not. Generally, she doesn't say anything to me. That's one thing I don't

I began to take a few pictures of Caroline. "You're making Caroline nervous," said John Walsh, a Secret Service agent.

Walsh is kind of a fanatic but I can generally handle him. "I don't think she minds," I said.

Caroline stopped playing and looked at me angrily. "Yes, I do mind!" she said.

like about Jackie. But anyhow I started taking pictures of her. And I saw the two Secret Servicemen with her. There was a new agent named Brian Keller just out of Notre Dame. I didn't know him. Then there was John Walsh, the chief of the eight agents who are assigned to watch Caroline and John. I've known Walsh for years.

"You're back again?" said Walsh. He's a beefy guy and he stood right in front of my camera blocking my view of Jackie. "Why don't you leave the lady alone? For four years you've been hounding her."

"What are you doing here?" I asked Walsh. "You're supposed to be guarding the children, not Jackie. That's what the law says. You guard the children." I'm a professional. I know my business.

"I'm taking care of her," said Walsh, and he pointed to Caroline, who was playing tennis on the court.

It was nice of him to point her out because until then I hadn't noticed Caroline. I put the lens of my camera right into one of the holes in the chain link fence. That's the way you get the best pictures shooting through fences. Don't hold the camera back from the fence or you'll get a lot of wire in the picture. I started taking pictures of Caroline playing tennis.

"You're making Caroline nervous," Walsh yelled at me.

Walsh is overemotional. He's a fanatic. He has been protecting those kids for so long that he's sort of a father to them. He protects them and that's good. He should protect them from danger. That's his job, but he goes too far. I'm not a danger to the children and he knows that. In fact, in a way, I help protect them. No one would try to kidnap them or anything while I'm around taking pictures.

I don't think I was bothering her. She seemed to be hitting the ball well. Of course, I don't know, I'm no tennis player.

"I'm not making her nervous," I told Walsh. "I don't think she minds." Caroline overheard us and stopped playing.

"Yes I do mind!" she said. And she looked right at me. I respect it when people talk to me.

Near Jackie was a new Secret Service agent, Brian Keller. I didn't realize she was paying any attention to me. And then it happened.

18

"I'm sorry, Caroline," I said. "I won't take any more pictures." And I didn't. Except for that picture of her saying she did mind. Well, at least I didn't take any more pictures of her at that moment.

I turned around and looked at Jackie. But she still wasn't looking at me. She was leaning against a tree. And I don't think she was paying any attention to me at all.

That's when it happened. Nothing like that had ever happened before and so I was taken completely by surprise. She walked over to agent Keller and said something to him. And then she started to run. Yes, run. She started to run across the field. She runs very nicely, very gracefully, like a deer. I know that she exercises a lot because I've taken pictures of her jogging and she is in good shape. She was running towards a police car. "Oh. Oh. She's gonna get the cops after me," I thought. But she didn't stop. She just kept running on past the police car towards the reservoir and the jogging path around it.

What made Jackie run? She had never done that to me before. In all the years of photographing her through airports and restaurants, across cow pastures in New Jersey, over the choppy blue waves off Skorpios, through the narrow streets of Capri, she had never once run away from me.

"But why?" I asked myself as I ran on the jogging path after her. "Why does she want me to chase her?" I think I knew even then that our relationship had reached a turning point, that after this there was no stopping, no going back. I knew that it was all going to be running from there on.

20 Jackie walked over to Keller and said something to him. Then she began to walk away.

Suddenly she started to run across the field. "She's gonna get the cops after me," I thought.

But Jackie ran right past the squad car. She picked up speed and kept on running toward the reservoir and the jogging track. I'm in terrible shape and was out of breath almost from the start; still I managed to follow her somehow.

23

Jackie Kennedy Onassis, the most desirable woman in
the world wanted to be chased by me, Ron Galella, the
paparazzo. I knew even then that there could be no
stopping, no turning back.

2

a day in the life of Jackie

Jackie. Jackie. Jackie. Everything depends on Jackie. Jackie is international, the biggest star all over the world. She doesn't have to do anything but step out of her door to make news. There is tremendous curiosity about Jackie. Everybody wants to know what Jackie is doing all the time. There are at least fifty fan magazines and they'll all buy pictures of Jackie. The *National Enquirer* will buy any new pictures of Jackie at any time. The fan magazines never get tired of her.

I didn't realize that at first. I didn't even start to take pictures of her until May 1967, when I got an assignment from *Motion Picture* magazine to take pictures of her at the Wildenstein Art Gallery in New York. I didn't even know where she lived then; another photographer had to lead me to her apartment building later on so that I could get some paparazzo shots of her.

My first pictures of Jackie weren't very good. I wasn't really inspired at first. But gradually Jackie became more and more a part of my life. I became more and more fascinated with her. It was a challenge to photograph her. More editors started to ask for her pictures. Her name started to show up more often on the request lists that *Time* and *Newsweek* send me every week. I began to realize that the media paid big money for good pictures of Jackie.

This all goes back to the very beginning. *Motion Picture* magazine gave me my first assignment to take pictures of Jackie, and I caught up with her at an opening at the Wildenstein art gallery in New York. They certainly weren't great pictures, but at least I learned where Jackie lived and got my first paparazzo shots of her, as she was escorted back to her apartment by Andre Meyer, a wall street financier who advises both Jackie and Ari.

I started to cover her and she began to notice me. She began to figure out that it was me who was getting all those pictures of her. One time I was waiting for her when she walked out of "21." She was very cool, very calm. I like that about Jackie. She's always very calm. She just walked over to me and grabbed my wrist and pinned me with her elbow against the side of her limousine. She has a good strong grip. She didn't seem very angry. If anything she seemed rather pleased. She just looked at me and said in her low voice:

"You've been hunting me for two months now."

"Yes," I said. "Yes, I have."

That was it. The first time we had ever spoken. She didn't say anything else. She just got into the limousine and drove off.

Why was I hunting her? It was more than just money. Was I falling in love with Jackie? No, not really. She's beautiful, but I go more for the Scandinavian type. The girl I'm going with now is Swedish-American. Maybe I'll get married before too long. I don't envy Ari for being married to Jackie. I'd like his money, but I couldn't handle Jackie. I get satisfaction out of taking good pictures of Jackie. She's not easy to photograph. She's a great challenge. She's very mobile, she would never stop and make it easy for photographers. Pictures— that's what I want from her.

A psychiatrist would probably say that I'm a voyeur or a Peeping Tom. I don't see it that way. I don't want to take pictures of Jackie nude. In hot pants, yes. In a bikini, sure. But not nude. I believe a girl can be more sexy with clothes on. The human face is the most important part of our body, because it expresses the gamut of human emotions, what we feel and think. Therefore I believe my favorite photo of Jackie is more sexy and in good taste than the nudes of Jackie that have been published. In one of the many friendly conversations I had with Ari, he said to me once, "You are like a baby compared to the paparazzi in Europe." Ari is right, the paparazzi in Europe are more aggressive: they have taken nudes and also crashed into a restaurant in Rome to get photos of Ari and Liz Taylor dining. I would never attempt to do this, because it is in bad taste. Photographers should have respect for privacy and decency when it is truly a private moment in a person's life. I want to take pictures of her the way she really lives her life from day to day. That's what people want to know about her. How does she dress? What does she eat? Where does she have her hair done? How does she get the groceries? What does she look like when she goes out for a walk?

What is a day in the life of Jackie like? I don't mean one actual day, but a sort of typical composite day.

If you wait outside of Jackie's building on a typical morning, you won't see anything until about 8:30. Then you will see John come out to go to school. Two Secret Servicemen drive John to Collegiate Boys School in one of the Secret Service's unmarked sedans. The two assigned agents remain in school until he is escorted back again. Two Secret Servicemen used to escort Caroline to Brearley in the same manner. Now she goes to boarding school at Concord Academy in Massachusetts. To be near her, Jackie has taken a house in Concord. Jackie and Caroline are very close. Caroline was 16 on

Ari, in my opinion, is a hard worker. Who wouldn't work hard for a million bucks a week? Since Ari usually goes off to work before Jackie leaves the apartment, he gets to keep the limousine for the whole day. George, the chauffeur (at the left in the top picture), goes with the limousine. I wish George would just keep going. He's been one of my toughest problems all along.

29

November 27, 1973, therefore is no longer protected by the Secret Service. Jackie likes to have her children lead private lives like normal children. She does not seem to realize they are special and the public is curious about them.

Ari, when he is in New York, comes next out of the house, at about 11:30. He gets into his personal limousine, which is always driven by George, the Greek chauffeur. I stay away from George. Some other chauffeurs will give you information, but not George. He never tells you anything, and if he's nearby when you're taking a picture of Jackie he'll hold your arm until she gets away. Once he even twisted the camera strap around my neck and almost choked me while Jackie was escaping into the limousine. George drives Ari to the Olympic Airlines Office, where Ari stays until 1 p.m. when he walks over to "21" for a steak sandwich. Sometimes Jackie meets Ari for lunch. Then Ari comes back to work at 2 p.m. and stays in the office until 7 or 8 p.m. Now and then Ari checks the construction of his monument in America, the Olympic Tower on Fifth Avenue. I think Ari works very hard. Well, I work hard, too, but I don't make a million bucks a week.

You almost never see Jackie come out in the morning and I don't blame her. But in the afternoon she goes out a lot,

On Mother's Day Jackie held this bouquet up in front of her face to block my picture. She has a lot of other tricks.

Here's a typical scene from a day in the life of
Jackie, as she emerges from her apartment
building. Her doorman is very loyal to her.
Here he's sort of running interference for her
—and giving me a tough look while he's at it.

particularly to shop. She buys brownies at Greenberg's on
86th Street and flowers at a little shop on 62nd Street. Once
I saw her buy some records by Santana, the California rock
and roll group, at Alexanders. She also shops at Blooming-
dales. But I think what she likes to do best is to buy clothes.
You have to be careful taking pictures of her because sometimes she doesn't like to be photographed doing these things
and she knows a lot of tricks for fooling photographers. If
she sees you, she'll put on sunglasses, or hold the flowers in
front of her face, or turn her head, or she'll even get so close
to you that you can't focus. She will even hide behind other
people. Most people wouldn't know that you can ruin a
picture by getting too close. Jackie's very clever. She used to
be an inquiring photographer herself, and I think that she still
is a frustrated photographer.

31

Just seeing Jackie leaving her apartment and getting in a limousine is kind of like watching a one-act play. When Jackie leaves the house in the morning she often draws a crowd.

This was the first time that Jackie claimed I flicked her with my camera straps. What do you think? Does she look to you like a woman who is being tortured?

33

Early in 1952, *The New York Times* columnist Arthur Krock, a close friend of Jackie, got her a job as Inquiring Camera Girl on the old *Washington Times-Herald*. Her training was a journalism course at George Washington University. Many times daily, she cornered a half-dozen strangers for her column, which takes a lot of chutzpah. She asked them human interest questions. She preferred doing columns on her favorite subjects such as ballet dancers or children, but she became noticed through public personalities (VIPs), one of which was Massachusetts Senator John Fitzgerald Kennedy. The rest is history. She also interviewed Vice President Nixon about the same time. *The Inquiring Camera Girl* by Jacqueline Bouvier was Jackie's first big contact with the outside world and she made the most of it.

As long as she stays in the apartment, Jackie is in another world as far as I'm concerned, because I would never sneak into the apartment to take a picture of her. That's private. But as soon as she walks out the front door of the building, she's in my world. That's public. Of course, I have to share her with a lot of other people. There's the doorman who leads the way to her limousine; there is often another photographer in the picture, and there is almost always some neighborhood clown or some passer-by trying to get into the act. When she gets into the limousine, she's on her own.

Sometimes I get into my car and follow her. One after-

I hid behind the counter at Bonwit Teller while Jackie bought a pair of slippers. Even though it looks as though she is looking right at me, Jackie didn't notice me until the next to the last picture.

Then she did what she usually does—she put on her sunglasses and walked out on me. But I was satisfied. I think I really did something worth while in showing that Jackie loves to shop as much as any woman—maybe more!

noon I saw her get into a rented limousine. Ari keeps their own limousine for himself. I followed her through traffic down Fifth Avenue until her car stopped in front of Bonwit Teller's and she got out. Then I was in a fix. She could let the chauffeur worry about the car, but I didn't have any chauffeur. I thought fast and stopped a teen-age kid on the street. "Here's five bucks," I told him. "Sit behind the wheel and pretend you're waiting for someone. This is a tow-away zone."

I rushed into the store and saw that Jackie had already gone upstairs. I couldn't go up after her because I was afraid that she might come down in another elevator. Then I saw her coming. Luckily, she didn't see me. And I was in luck again because instead of walking out she stopped at the shoe

This little scene took place on another day. Jackie took refuge from me in this Cyclax Shop. I don't know who this woman in the doorway is, but Jackie undoubtedly told her to look out and see if there were any photographers waiting, meaning me! Hello there!

counter. I squirmed into a space behind the counter and hid behind a display.

"You can't go in there," one of the sales ladies told me.

"It's all right," I said. "I'm her personal photographer." Which was true in a way.

The sales people didn't make any big fuss over her. And she was very ladylike. She didn't demand any special attention or get mad when other customers looked over her shoulder to see what she was buying. Of course she probably would not have liked it if she had known I was taking pictures. She looked at different shoes and then asked, like any other woman would have, if she could try on a pair of golden slippers. It wasn't exactly like any other woman. When she decided she wanted the slippers, she didn't take out

On Saturdays Ari usually takes Jackie to lunch at P. J. Clarke's. On this occasion he had trouble getting a cab, but he still turned down my offer to give him and Jackie a lift. Imagine what would happen to me if he actually accepted my offer: I would have fallen over in a faint!

The shots above show one way of catching Jackie in action: you call Kenneth's and ask what time her appointment is. That way you'll be sure to meet her.

At the left are more shots of Jackie and Ari walking near P. J. Clarke's. Ari doesn't seem too friendly in spite of my generous offer to give him a lift.

any cash or even sign the charge slip. She just told the saleswoman to send them. And she didn't have to show any identification or tell her whom to charge, of course.

Sometimes, if I miss her at her building, I drive past some of her favorite spots like Cyclax where she goes for her facials a couple of times a week, or Kenneth's where she has her hair done. If I see a limousine with a Z license plate (Z means it's rented) out in front, then I get suspicious that it might be Jackie. And so I ask the chauffeur. Never ask, "Who are you driving today?" because he'll just say, "Oh, some business-man. You wouldn't be interested." Always be positive. Say, "Oh, you're driving Jackie today." You can tell by the expression on his face whether he is or not.

As I said, though, Jackie gets smarter all the time. When she found out that I was following the limousine she started to take cabs quite often. Cabs are difficult to follow. They all look alike and when they weave in and out of traffic they lose you easily.

Of course, taking cabs can backfire on her. One Saturday Jackie and Ari went to P.J. Clarke's, which is one of their favorite spots to go for lunch on weekends. After lunch they came out and ducked into the King Karol Record Store. I went in but Jackie had the manager throw me out before I could take a picture. So I took one from outside. Soon, Ari came out and tried to get a cab. But he couldn't. Just like anybody else he was standing there on the corner with all the "off duty" cabs whizzing by. I guess none of the drivers recognized him. Well, actually, I heard he's not such a hot tipper, so they weren't missing much.

I stepped up to Ari and I said, "I have my car here. Can I give you a lift?"

"No," he said. "We would just like to ride in peace."

Finally, a cab stopped, Jackie came out of the store, where she was waiting for Ari to get the cab, and they drove off.

To figure out in advance what Jackie intends to do during the day, it helps to have an insider. Once I had a real insider. One evening I was waiting outside Jackie's building and was just about to leave when this nice-looking girl came out. I offered her a ride and she accepted. She told me her name was Greta Neilsen and she was Norwegian; but when she told me, in the car, that she was Jackie's maid I forgot all about her other good points. All that mattered was that she could tell me things about Jackie. I dated her for weeks and she would tell me such things as when Jackie was going to have her hair done. And so you know what I did? I called up Kenneth's pretending that I was on Jackie's staff and said that I wanted to check on what time her appointment was. They told me, and so the next day when Jackie showed up, so did I.

Actually Greta hurt me as much as she helped me. One

This is Greta Neilson, Jackie's maid—until she met me. Jackie and the Secret Service gave Greta the credit for all of my successes, but in the long run I think Greta hurt me almost as much as she helped me.

night I took her and her girl friend Olga to a premiére. The two of them were laughing all the way through it. Later I found out why. Jackie and Ari had gone to the airport while we were in the theatre, and I missed what could have been a great take.

And then one day, while I was standing outside the building waiting for Jackie to come home, Greta happened to come along and we started talking. All of a sudden Jackie appeared and caught us together. I was really embarrassed. It was about the only time I've ever been embarrassed in front of Jackie. It was all over then, of course, for Greta. One of the Secret Servicemen later confronted her and accused her of giving me information. Jackie called her in and fired her. Greta told me later that it was the only time that Jackie had ever spoken to her. She simply told her: "You may leave now."

So much for Greta. Insiders can be useful but what I really rely on are my own observations, instincts, knowledge and my skills like a detective. One Sunday afternoon I was waiting outside the apartment when I heard a parade coming up Fifth Avenue, but still a long way off. I thought to

This series is the result of a kind of inspiration. There was a parade going by their building and it suddenly struck me that Ari had probably never seen a parade in New York before and would be curious. I don't think I could ever get a take like this again in a hundred years. I was lying on my back in Central Park when Jackie appeared first at the balcony of her apartment. Then Ari showed up and finally I was lucky enough to get this picture of the two of them together.

myself: "Oh, I'll bet that Ari has never seen a parade in America before. When he hears that noise, he'll probably look out the window."

I was very tired. A paparazzo has to keep long hours and so I stretched out my raincoat in the park across the street and lay down. I told some kids who were playing there I would give five bucks to the first one who saw Jackie or Ari peeping through the window. I trust kids more than older people. They tell the truth. A few minutes later, sure enough, both Jackie and Ari came out on their balcony to see the

"Follow that woman." I told the cab driver. For once Jackie's instincts were all wrong. Instead of turning away, she made a mistake and turned right toward me.

parade. I just lay there and snapped the pictures. I sold the pictures to *Oggi,* the Italian magazine, and to many other publications all over the world.

Many times Jackie likes to end the afternoon by walking or jogging around the reservoir or just strolling on Madison Avenue. One afternoon I was in Central Park across from Jackie's apartment with Joy Smith. Joy is one of those pretty girls you are sometimes lucky enough to meet in a job like this. She had just graduated from the University of Iowa Drama School and had come to New York to be an actress and a model. A mutual friend introduced us and I took her to the park to shoot some test photographs that she could use for her modeling portfolio.

As we were leaving the park, I caught sight of Jackie, wearing tie-dye pants and a drab gray sweater, sneaking out the side entrance. The doorman had warned her that I was across the street.

"That couldn't be Jackie," said Joy, surprised but excited too. "Dressed like that?"

"Yeah, that's her," I said. "Come on, before she gets away."

We followed her over to Madison and I had to think, "How am I going to catch up with her, to get in front of her? If she hears someone running behind her, she'll see me." So with Joy still with me, I hailed a cab.

"Follow that woman," I told the driver and pointed at Jackie.

I told the driver to slow down and I opened the window as we rode alongside her. I started taking pictures. She must have heard the clicking of the camera. But for once, Jackie's instincts were all wrong. I fooled her. Instead of turning away, she turned right toward me, and as she did I got what I think is the most beautiful picture of her I've ever taken. She was walking in full stride, half turned toward me with the breeze blowing wisps of hair across her face *spontaneously— she looks very sexy.* It was beautiful, one of the classics of paparazzo photography. The picture I had been looking for! I'm so proud of it I asked my publisher to run the picture at the beginning of this book.

Joy, a camera buff, photographed us together. She did, very professionally. It really shows what I'm like in action. Incidentally, I don't grunt, the way Jackie said I did in court. I may breathe heavily sometimes when I'm moving fast, but I don't grunt.

"Are you pleeeeeased with yourself?" Jackie asked, as Joy and I finished and walked away.

I was pleased and said "thank you" and just kept walking. The shadows were getting longer and the light was fading. No more pictures now. It was the end of the day for Jackie.

But ahead of us was the long, exciting night.

I handed Joy one of my cameras. I didn't know what she could do with it, but it was an opportunity I couldn't pass up. Here was a chance to get that picture so many editors all over the world were crying for.

This pretty much wrapped up the long sequence of shots I took of Jackie from the cab and while I was walking along behind her. I was satisfied. A very productive day was over —and an exciting night was about to begin.

3

a night in the life of Jackie

Did Jackie use judo on a *Daily News* photographer when she was coming out of the movie *I am Curious (Yellow)?* In court, during the trial, Jackie did admit that she was very angry at the four or five photographers that were at the theater. I was not there. Recently, I asked the *Daily News* photographer what happened that night. He said that he tripped on the sidewalk and was not flipped. The press distorted this to make a sensational story out of it. I believe Jackie does not like distortions like the ones the press writes about her, and I don't blame her. But what does she have against photographers who record an authentic representation of what is before them? Jackie said during the trial that none of the many photographs I had taken of her embarrassed her. Then what disturbs her about photographers? Besides the gossip written about her, I believe she envies my success as a paparazzo: you see, Jackie never made it as a photographer!

Some photographers, like the daily newspaper photographers, just wait around for some publicity agent to call and say, "Hey, Jackie's eating at our restaurant," or "Guess what? Jackie went into our theatre." I don't work that way very much and here are the reasons: By the time you get to the restaurant or the theatre the publicity agent has called in so many photographers that you can't get an exclusive. Or Jackie might have left already. Or she might suspect a tipoff is in the works and so she is ready to hide her face or take a powder. Also, some restaurants and theatres have no publicity agents to rely on.

I get my best results from doing research, from knowing my subject and from starting at the source. I always ask myself, "I wonder what Jackie's doing tonight?" That doesn't mean that I follow Jackie every night, but if I think there's a good chance that she might be going out, I want to be there.

What is a typical night in the life of Jackie like?

Actually, Jackie doesn't go out at night as much as people might think. When Ari isn't in New York—he comes in for two or three weeks at a time and then goes back to Athens or Paris or London for a few months—Jackie spends most nights at home. I don't know what she does on those nights. Maybe she watches television or maybe she reads books or magazines.

And so the first problem is to figure out whether she is going out at all. There are some clues. If I see her getting her hair done during the day, then I'm pretty sure she's going out that night. If Ari is in town, I figure that they might be going out to dinner because Ari likes good food. If Ari isn't in town, and I see a limousine pull up about an hour before the nightly Olympic Airlines flight from Europe, it's a good bet that Ari is on it, and that Jackie is going out to the airport to meet him.

But there are several other sources of information. I keep close watch on the gossip columns—Leonard Lyons and Earl

May 15, 1968: This was the first time that I met and photographed Aristotle Onassis. He was alone and appeared very suave and sophisticated. It was a party given by Margot Fonteyn at the El Morocco; Aristotle Onassis is very good friends with her and Rudolph Nureyev.

Wilson in the *Post*, Suzy Knickerbocker in the *News*, the "eye" page in *Women's Wear Daily*.

In that way I get some pretty good leads. If the Royal Ballet is in town, Jackie will probably go at least once because both she and Ari are very good friends of Rudolph Nureyev, the lead dancer. If her sister, Lee Radziwill, is in town there's a very good chance she is going out to dinner or the theatre with her. Actually, Lee is more outgoing than Jackie. I check the theatre directory and try to figure out what she might be going to see. She doesn't like anything too far out, nothing off-Broadway or anything like that. I followed her to *Hair* once, but that was about the most unusual

Jackie at the opera . . . and at the ballet.

I check the theatre directory and try to figure out what she might
be going to see. This time it was *Forty Carats*.

thing I ever followed her to and even *Hair* was on Broadway.
Usually she likes to see something like *Forty Carats* or
Company.

If I decide that she probably is going out that night, I try
to be at her apartment by 7 p.m. Jackie doesn't know it, but
I can tell where she's going by what time the limousine
arrives. If it comes at 7, I know she's leaving early to go to
the theatre in time for the 7:30 p.m. curtain. If the limousine
comes at 7:30, that means the ballet at 8 p.m. If the limousine comes about 8 or 8:30, I know they're going out to
dinner. If no limousine shows up by 10 p.m., I decide that
they're not going out at all, and so I check a couple of
premières or clubs for other celebrities, and then I go home.

But Jackie can fool you. She is always full of surprises.
That's what I like so much about her. She's always doing
something unexpected. She is a real challenge to any photojournalist, even a paparazzo.

One night I showed up a little late, and one of the
doormen in the neighborhood told me that Jackie had gone
out alone and the limousine had made a left turn on 84th
Street. That could only mean one thing, I thought. Straight
down Fifth Avenue would have meant dinner or the theatre.
A right turn through the park would have meant the ballet at
Lincoln Center. A left could only mean a trip to the airport
to pick up Ari, particularly since she was alone. Jackie almost
never goes out alone at night except to pick up Ari.

I drove the 20 miles to Kennedy Airport, but no Jackie. I
couldn't find her anywhere. I was worried. Where could she
be? That left turn had to mean a trip to the airport. But
where was she? Had she taken a plane herself? No. That
couldn't be. The doorman would have mentioned luggage.

51

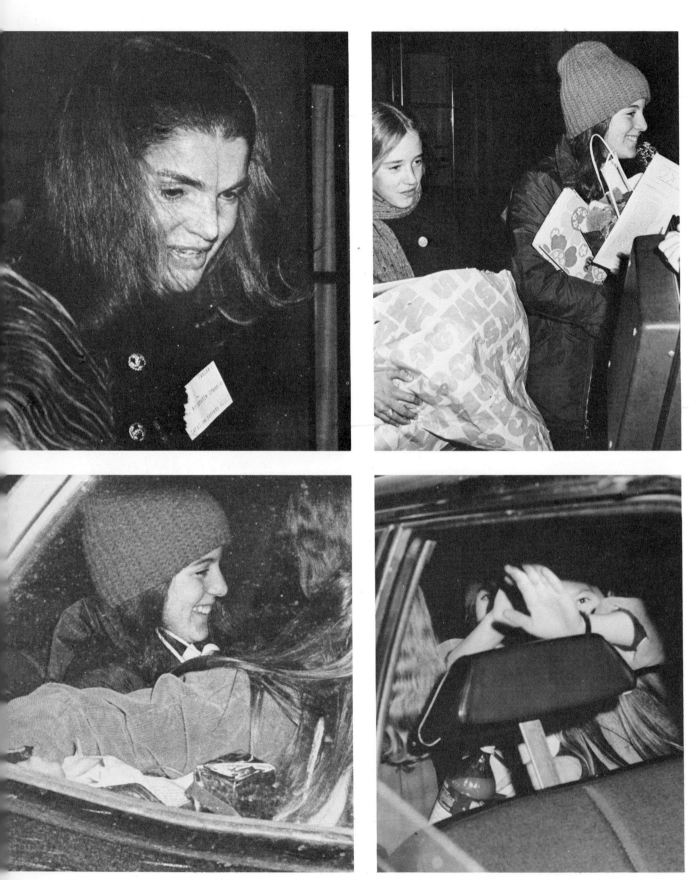

Like all the other parents, she was wearing a name card
with her name and Caroline's. Who needed a name card
to identify her? Maybe somebody from Mars.

52

Then, I remembered. Caroline's school, Brearley at 83rd Street and East End Avenue. She would have taken a left to get there, too. Could it be? I had to take the chance. I got back into town as fast as I could and stopped in front of the school. I was right the second time around. She was just coming out of a dinner for the school parents. Like all the other parents, she was wearing a name card with her name and her child's, "Mrs. Aristotle Onassis, Caroline Kennedy, Table #1."

Where else would you put Jackie but table #1? But who needed a name card to identify her? Maybe somebody from Mars. Anyway, I got some good pictures that night.

And then there was the night she went to see *Two Gentlemen of Verona*. That was a close call. I almost missed that one. I showed up at her apartment building late in the afternoon. It was winter and dark already, and as I got close I could see flashes of light. Up close I saw two other photographers taking pictures of Jackie by flash. She was walking the dog. It was very unusual to see Jackie walking the dog, and her clothes were very bizarre. Tie dye pants, windbreaker,

If I'd known she was planning to go to the theatre later this same night, I probably wouldn't have alerted her by taking this picture.

53

Even though I missed Jackie's entrance, I caught her at the Playbill bar during intermission, and coming out of the Russian Tea Room with Peter Duchin after a late supper.

white gloves, sneakers, sunglasses and a bandana around her head. I was so interested in taking a picture of her like that, walking the dog, that I didn't notice that her bandana was hiding some special hairdo. That would have been a give-away that she was going out that evening. Usually, I'm pretty sharp about those things, but that night I didn't notice.

Instead I went off to get dinner and some rest because I had planned to go to the premiere of *Two Gentlemen of Verona* that night. I didn't expect to see Jackie, because Jackie almost never goes to premieres, but I hoped to get some other celebrities. I showed up at the theatre late because I overslept in the Croydon Hotel lobby. Other photographers told me Jackie was already there! That was a surprise. She had come with Peter and Cheray Duchin and with Michael Forrestal, a lawyer friend. I wished I had known she was coming, I probably wouldn't have taken pictures of her walking the dog because then she would be alerted. All in all, I still got some very good takes. Even though I missed their entrance, I got pictures of them having a drink at the Playbill bar during intermission, and leaving the theatre, and I even got pictures of them later coming out of the Russian Tea Room, where they had gone for supper after the play..

I would have taken even more pictures, but I guess Jackie got into a bad mood late in the evening. I was following the limousine home after the supper at the Russian Tea Room when it stopped at a traffic light. I stopped behind it. The chauffeur got out and walked back to my car. I rolled down the window.

"She says she knows who you are," the chauffeur told me, "and she wants you to stop following her or she'll call the police."

"Okay," I said, "I'm leaving."

When Ari is in town the two of them, Jackie and Ari, go out a lot, to "21", El Morroco, the Casino Russe (now the Blue Angel) and when they were first married, although not so much anymore, to La Côte Basque for dinner. I spent a lot of winter nights trying to keep warm outside La Côte Basque. One of the worst things about being a paparazzo is the waiting. Even when you are successful in following Jackie to a place, you still have to wait. Here's the reason. Because she's going inside and you're staying outside, the only picture you can get of her is her back. To get her face you have to wait until she comes out, and when Jackie and Ari go to dinner at La Côte Basque it can mean a three- or four-hour wait. Once I took some pictures of her through the window at La Côte Basque. She was smoking; for the most part I don't like to take pictures of Jackie eating. She's so super glamorous that people don't think of her doing things ordinary people do, like eating. Anyhow, La Côte Basque wouldn't let me in to take pictures.

And so I wait outside. Sometimes, while Jackie is eating I go to have a bowl of lentil soup or a corned-beef sandwich and coffee at a Greek coffee shop. And sometimes I sleep in my car. But the easiest way to pass the time is to talk to another paparazzo. A few years ago I met a young guy named Tom Wargacki outside the Plaza Hotel waiting to get a look at Liz Taylor. He was just a fan then and I asked him to hold my car for me while I went to get some pictures of Liz. He did. After that I started to see Tom more and more often, waiting for Liz or waiting for Jackie and we became good friends. He was just a student then, studying photography at the New York Institute of Photography. But I taught him how to be a paparazzo, and now he's a good paparazzo.

Tom is successful, perhaps not as successful as I am. He has an English wife who is a big help. Tom brought his wife with

Mid-November, 1970: Jackie, Ari, Prince Stanislas and Princess Lee Radziwill and Pierre Salinger had dinner together at La Côte Basque. A chauffeur carries the umbrella.

him when he went to take some pictures of Jackie's cousins and aunt in East Hampton. She did all the talking and so Jackie's cousins and aunt thought Tom was taking pictures for an English society paper. They didn't know that Tom was really taking pictures for the *National Enquirer.*

But Tom, at that time, didn't have a car, which is a big disadvantage for a paparazzo, and so sometimes he rode along with me. While we sat outside La Côte Basque waiting for Jackie to come out, we talked. Mostly business. We talked about what Jackie was eating. I'm not envious of her that way. Maybe I think like a peasant, but I think in those expensive restaurants you pay for the name and you pay for the service, but you can get as good a meal elsewhere for much less. We also talked about what Jackie was wearing and what kind of problems her clothes are going to present for the pictures. Jackie wears black too much at night and we don't like that. Black at night is black against black and you can't get any good separation.

And then Tom and I talked about how much pictures of Jackie are selling for. He told me where he sold his last take and I told him where I sold mine. We're competitors, in a way, but we also cooperate a lot. The market for pictures of Jackie is so big that neither one of us could flood it and ruin the other, and helping each other has a lot of advantages. For example, when Jackie comes out of La Côte Basque, Tom stands on one side of the door and I stand on the other. If she turns away from me, she faces Tom; if she turns away from Tom, she faces me.

A fellow paparazzo, Tom Wargacki, poses for me with his English wife.

Pictures of Jackie fetch a better price than pictures of anyone else in the world. The only pictures that would pay better, if anyone could get them, might be exclusive pictures of Howard Hughes, but probably only the first pictures. After that Howard Hughes wouldn't be worth much. Jackie, on the other hand, never depreciates. The prices you get for Jackie pictures depend on where you sell them. Newspapers don't pay very much and so you can pretty much forget about newspapers since most have staffers, except for the *National Enquirer*, which will pay $350 for a page one of Jackie.

Fan magazines pay a minimum of $25 for a small black and white gossip column shot but $300 to $500 for a color cover. *Time* and *Newsweek* are mostly interested in single pictures and they will pay a minimum of $50 a picture. Women's magazines, like *McCall's* and *Cosmopolitan,* pay about the same. *Life* pays the best prices. I once sold a cover and inside spread to *Life* for $5,000, the best sale I ever made. They gave me $1,500 for the cover because it was Jackie. They usually pay only $1,000. And they paid me $3,600 for the pictures they used inside. The foreign market can be very good, too. I have sold pictures to publications in Hong Kong, Japan, Australia and practically everywhere else. But the Italian and German magazines are the ones that are most interested in Jackie and they pay well. *Stern* and *Burda Publications* of Germany paid just as well as *Life.*

After dinner Jackie and Ari sometimes go to one of their two favorite clubs, Hippopotamus or Raffles, or sometimes, on a nice summer night, Ari sends the chauffeur home and they go for a walk. Tom and I trailed them while they looked in the window of a Russian antique store on 59th Street.

"There's your friend again," Jackie said to Ari in a sarcastic way.

She meant me, but she didn't look at me. That's something I don't like about Jackie. She almost never talks to me directly. What would I talk about if Jackie ever did talk to me? If I were invited inside to have dinner with her at La Côte Basque? I'm not sure. I'd probably talk to her about photography and her beauty. As I said before, I think she's a frustrated photographer. I'd certainly ask her why she never talked to me before.

"Why don't you do like in Europe?" Ari said to me. "Take a couple of pictures and then go away."

Well, I don't agree with him that that's the way they do things in Europe, but Tom and I did what he asked. We took a couple of pictures and then went away. One of the rules of being a good paparazzo is, "Never stay around when people are getting annoyed. Go away. Cool it."

I said that I never follow Jackie into the restaurant to get pictures of her eating. There was one big exception to that,

Tom and I trailed them to 59th Street. 'Why don't you do like in Europe?'' Ari said to me. ''Take a couple of pictures and then go away.''

the night I took on what I call my *Mission Impossible.* It was a winter night, pretty cold, and Tom and I were both sitting in my car outside the apartment when we saw the limousine pull up.

I had the feeling that something big was up that night, but I wasn't quite sure what. Jackie and Ari got into the limousine and the limousine took off headed downtown. I expected it to stop somewhere in the 50's for La Côte Basque or "21", but it just kept going. Then I knew my hunch was right. Something big was up.

It was good that Tom was with me because when we got farther and farther downtown, it was harder and harder for me to drive and watch the limousine at the same time. We kept turning and winding down narrow streets, through dark places with strange names I had never heard before. Again and again I thought we lost them and then Tom spotted the limousine again. And then suddenly we stopped. I realized that we were in Chinatown.

We stopped in front of an ordinary-looking Chinese restau-

After stopping to ask for directions, the chauffeur took Ari, Jackie and a group of their friends to this Chinese restaurant in lower Manhattan. After pushing my camera bag across the floor with my foot, I hid behind the coat rack for forty-five minutes.

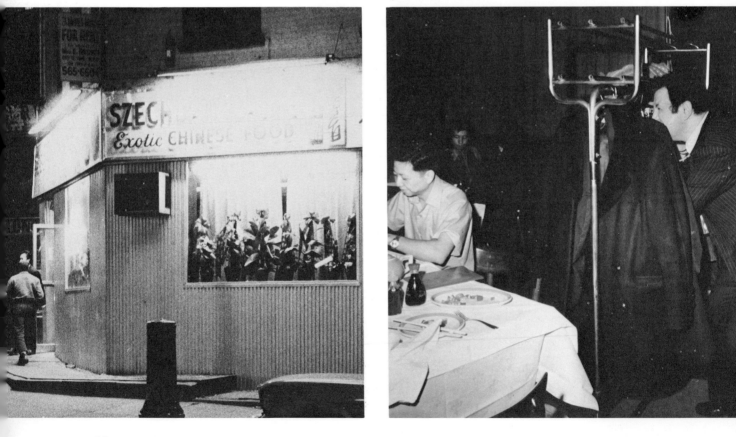

rant and Jackie and Ari were going inside. I started to get excited. This was it. A chance to get a picture of Jackie eating with chopsticks. I knew that Jackie sometimes ate Chinese food but nobody had ever taken a picture of her with chopsticks.

"Tom," I said. "I'm going in."

"Don't risk it," Tom said, "It's too small, too intimate. You'll get caught."

The Chinese owner noticed me through the window and came outside. He was so eager for publicity that he invited me inside. This was very unusual. Ordinarily, I have to persuade the restaurant owner to let me in. But in this case I had to warn the owner to be cautious, that we had to be careful because Jackie and Ari are shy and sometimes do not like to have their pictures taken.

He took me inside. It was a very small restaurant and he put me at a table that was close to theirs. Too close. They were sitting almost next to me, Jackie and Ari, along with Doris Duke, I. M. Pei, the architect who designed the John F.

The sound of my Nikon was covered by the radio, which the proprietor had agreed to turn up for me. Thus I got the first pictures of Jackie eating with chopsticks.

Kennedy Library at Harvard, his wife and some other people I didn't recognize. It was a great scene, but I was too close to take pictures without being noticed.

In fact I was so close I had to hold the menu in front of my face to keep from being recognized. When the waiter came over and asked what I wanted, I just pointed at Jackie's table and said, "I'll have whatever they're having."

All through the special Szechuan meatball soup I kept asking myself, "How am I going to get the pictures?" Then it came to me. The coat rack.

It was a cold night and so there were plenty of coats hanging in the rack. Enough to hide me. The available light, fluorescent, was good enough so that I wouldn't have to use the flash with Tri-X film. It should work, I thought. I called the owner over. I asked him to turn up the radio to drown out any noise that the clicking of the Nikon camera might make. And while he covered my movements I tiptoed to the coat rack and slipped in among the coats. I poked the lens of the camera out and just started clicking away. I got everything I wanted, including a picture of Jackie eating with

When I first came in I had been sitting almost right next to Jackie, Ari, Doris Duke, the Rutherfords and Mr. and Mrs. I. M. Pei. The pictures of Aristotle Onassis smoking a cigar won me a prize with the Cigar Institute of America.

chopsticks. She looked very good, very coordinated. I slipped out of the coat rack and sneaked out of the restaurant before dessert, and although Jackie saw me outside the restaurant later taking pictures of her and her friends, she never realized that I had been in the coat rack. At least she didn't realize it until the pictures appeared in many newspapers and magazines.

After a night like that I'm tired. I figure Jackie and Ari are tired, too, but I try to save enough energy to go back to the apartment for that one last picture of Ari sending the chauffeur home. I think Ari pays his staff very well and if it's George, his personal chauffeur, he doesn't tip, but if it's a rented limousine, he gives the chauffeur a tip.

Not a big tip. Ari got mad at me once when I took a picture of him giving a two-dollar tip to the chauffeur. The bills were folded over so it looked like four dollars. The chauffeur left with a disgusted look.

And then Jackie and Ari go inside to their apartment. The end of a typical night on the town. Jackie has stopped running for today. I wish her pleasant dreams. I really do.

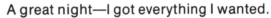

A great night—I got everything I wanted.

Ari apparently isn't a big tipper; he got mad at me when I took a picture of him giving a chauffeur two dollars. The chauffeur left with a disgusted look.

4

what makes Ron run?

Why did I become a paparazzo?

That's a question people ask me all the time. That's a question my mother asked me after I was beaten up covering Richard Burton and Elizabeth Taylor in Mexico, and again after Brando broke my jaw in New York City.

I come from a typical Italian family in the Bronx. My father came to this country from Potenza, a small town near Naples. First he was a piano maker and later he became a casket maker. My mother is Italian-American. Her parents came from Italy, but she herself was born in Hoboken, New Jersey. My three brothers and I are mechanically inclined since my father's tools were always around the house. One of my brothers, the most industrious one, is a building contractor. Another one is a tile setter—I was a tile setter myself for awhile—and the third brother is an electrician. My sister is married to a waiter at "21," but otherwise nobody else in the family is in the jet set.

I guess I was a little different from the others from the start. All the other children were named for the saints. But I was the best-looking of the boys and I was named for Ronald Coleman. My mother loved glamour. She was Americanized. She liked to spend money and buy clothes. But my father was very serious and frugal. He worked hard and didn't like to go out and spend a lot of money. There was a lot of fighting, a lot of conflict between my mother and my father. And there was a lot of sibling rivalry. It was very noisy in my house. You had to be loud to make yourself heard and that's why I still speak loudly today. And that's why I don't go out with Italian girls. Too noisy. I've had enough of that. That's ·one thing about Jackie—she speaks softly.

I don't really know too much about Jackie's childhood. But even though we were both born about the same time and we are both Catholic, we really don't have very much in common. She was brought up to be modest, I grew up wild. I did not have it easy. I started working part-time when I was twelve. To make money I used to go "junking." I would swipe the drains from the roofs of houses that were being built and then I would sell the copper. The North Bronx was like the country then. All the Italians had gardens and at night there was singing and serenading and my father used to make home-made wine. And we had tomato fights.

But I was different from the others. I had a lot of imagination, and from the time I was very young my heroes were the great romantic stars of fiction, like D'Artagnan of *The Three*

My father, Vincenzo, was born in Italy and was a hard-working cabinet maker who had only two jobs in America, that of piano maker and that of casket maker.

66

My mother, Michelina, is an Italian-American dressmaker. Like most Italians she is a good cook.

Musketeers and Don Quixote and Cyrano de Bergerac. I was artistic. I think most people don't use the creative talents they have. Instead of doing something on their own, making something with their own hands or minds, they would rather watch television. But I'm creative and I use my talents. In this world, there is nothing more abundant than talent and nothing scarcer than perseverance—ambition, industry and faith (in one's self). Energy or drive is the most important ingredient for success in a photographer or in any line of work. Most people do not want to work. The world is full of pretenders, bluffers, loafers in disguise, bunglers and inefficient people. It just cries out for the real thing. The real thing is the photographer or person with the imagination to conceive—and the will to do. King Arthur said "make the world other," so that must be applied to our modern world today. To change the world—to make it better, each in our own way. Each of us must have this will to act on faith to work intelligently toward our ideal. To succeed as a freelancer, you must gamble by investing your energy, time and money to produce pictures with taste or good ideas on "speculation" or independent production. You will never make it by waiting for assignments. Today, many big-name pros don't even get assignments, even they have to rely on their own initiative. The formula for success, if there is one, is:

Energy plus taste and ideas equals success; or
Energy plus taste equals success; or
Energy plus ideas equals success.

Note the common denominator is *energy*.

Ideally, a professional photographer starts out with a preconceived picture idea or theme; then he proceeds to produce that picture. It's not easy to do because of the many uncontrollable factors that get in the way, or can go wrong. The professional does not get discouraged easily—he perseveres. He aims for his ideal or perfection, even though he does not always attain it. This is the reason most pros shoot a lot of film. Once while leaving La Côte Basque one evening, Jackie was with Ari and F. D. Roosevelt, Jr., who said "No judo tonight!" to freelancer Tom Wargacki and myself while we took pictures. I was disguised with a hat and mustache (see photos). Jackie remarked in a very cheerful mood, "They never have enough." Paul Newman sometimes makes a similar remark to photographers when he is photographed. My answer to these remarks are: actors are allowed to bury their mistakes during their rehearsals; doctors bury their mistakes in the cemetery; artists bury their mistakes by painting over; so why shouldn't we photographers bury our mistakes on our contact proof sheets? (The photographer must take another exposure when he makes a mistake, technical or otherwise.) Besides, editors want to see a wide selection of expressions and compositions in pictures. So why not?

67

My three brothers are Louie, Nickie, and Vinnie. I have one sister, Camille. All are married. I never married. I've been preoccupied with my career in photography.

Most people think that a paparazzo is a no-good, just a bum who has a lot of nerve and a lot of patience, but no talent. But that's not true, not in my case anyway. For me paparazzo photography is a creative life. It's my way of expressing life, of getting life on film, just like a painter or a sculptor or a writer expresses life. I don't live in a vacuum. I relate all the arts to photography. I learned composition from painting, lighting from the theater (lighting is the most important tool the photographer has; with light, he draws with and expresses the mood of his picture), what the human body can do from ballet; from music I relate color and tonal gradations to the musical range of a piano. The more control I have of my medium, the more of an artist I become.

Even when I was very young I was creative. I remember that in high school we had a masquerade and I made myself a swashbuckler costume. I dyed a pair of longjohns black to make the tights; then I made the boots out of the sleeves of an old leather jacket, and a sword out of a broomstick and used a metal ashtray for the foil. It turned out good. And then after high school I had a job making ceramic sculpture

I began my career in photography in the U.S.A.F., when I enlisted during the Korean war. Ever since then I've been hooked on it.

Here, at four years old, I was rather shy with the photographer. My brother Vinnie is with me.

and lamp bases at the Associated American Artists. It was at this time that I sculptured my childhood heroes.

During the Korean Conflict, I enlisted in the Air Force where I got my start in photography. I graduated from Lowry Air Force Base School of Photography and Camera Repair. Since I was stationed in Florida, I used to take pictures of the beautiful girls in Miami in my spare time. I was really shooting paparazzo style then, too, and so I guess I've been a paparazzo for as long as I've been a photographer.

One thing I learned in the Air Force: if you want to accomplish anything, like getting a "hop," you must go to the decision-making ranks such as the pilots. I had no trouble getting "hops" everywhere. In the Air Force I became a jet-setter. Not only did I photograph news for the base newspaper, but I made news on the front page by "hopping" 20,000 miles by military aircraft to nine European countries while taking pictures. This occurred while on a 45-day furlough. I gave myself a photo assignment to see if I could make it as a paparazzo. I started hitchhiking from McCoy Air Force Base, Orlando, Florida, where I was stationed. I took

One of my heroes is Cyrano de Bergerac. I sculptured this when I did ceramics for the Association of American Artists.

In the Air Force I was asked to decorate the mess hall. So I painted this mural depicting the interdependence and team work of airmen.

Another of my heroes is D'Artagnan. I also did this when I was working for the Association of American Artists.

In high school I made this swashbuckler costume for a masquerade.

over 1,000 photos, some of beautiful girls. Expenses were practically nil, only $150 was spent on minor travel, hotels and food. That's when I first realized the "How to Succeed" technique—which was to go to the decision-making level of an organization and avoid the lower ranks. I was to later use this direct approach with the celebrities by avoiding the lower ranks (agents and bodyguards) if at all possible. On the other hand, nonorganization, independent low-rank people like doormen, chauffeurs, secretaries, and such, can sometimes be useful for valuable information.

After my service in the Air Force, I went to the Art Center College of Design in Los Angeles, graduating with a Bachelor of Professional Arts degree in Photojournalism. In Hollywood, I used to give myself paparazzo homework assignments. I would send myself to crash premiere parties. That was back in 1952 and I remember that I photographed Frank Sinatra, William Holden, Vivian Blaine, Gregory Peck and other stars that way. They were really my first paparazzi subjects and I've been at it ever since.

You have to remember that paparazzo is just a technique. Basically, it is the technique of catching people off guard, when they are not posing or putting on an act for the camera. Sometimes you have to go to great lengths to get pictures like that. Usually I don't ask a star's permission to take pictures. The reasons I don't are many: one, it will destroy the spontaneous, off-guard mood by getting a posed shot if they do consent. Second, it's too easy for the star to say "no" because of many excuses, such as their hair not being combed or their make-up not right or that they just have no time. Jackie testified in court that when she was a photographer for a Washington newspaper, she would always ask permission. Well, that was her approach. For me it doesn't work. It's not my style. But the technique is not the final objective. The final objective is to get the good picture, the meaningful and artistic picture. I'm a good photographer first and foremost and paparazzi is just an approach for getting pictures of celebrities the way I like to shoot them. I like to make the stars look beautiful, but beautiful in a natural, on-the-spot way. That's the way people like to see the stars, and Jackie is a star . . . the brightest of them all, even though she is not a movie star.

But there are other things I like about being a paparazzo, too. It gives me a chance to be an actor and a detective as well as a photographer. For example, I learned from going to these premiere parties that I had to play a role, that I had to look and act as though I belonged. I carried a lot of cameras and dressed to fit the occasion. But most important, I walked with authority. The guards figured that I looked so obvious I must belong, so they let me in. If I had carried just one camera and tried to be inconspicuous they would have fig-

I carry an assortment of wigs, mustaches and hats in my car for disguises. It helps with someone like Jackie who knows me.

ured that I was some paparazzo trying to crash the party and would have thrown me out.

To be a better actor and to try to understand my subjects better I studied acting at the Pasadena Playhouse. I didn't do too well because I'll never be able to get rid of this heavy Bronx accent. But it gave me more of a feeling of what it is like to be an actor—what it is like to be on the other side of the camera. It's scary to be out there on the stage alone.

In 1963 I worked as a lab technician in the TIME-LIFE lab and learned much about printing there. Since then I have always done my own printing in my darkroom. While at the lab, I continued photographing celebrities at Broadway openings and movie premieres. As a freelancer, you must come up with a good picture and also be able to sell it. Unlike staffers who put in their 8 hours and go home, I usually put in 80 hours a week. But for me it's my life work and I love it.

The money in this job can be very good. The media place a high value on the type of pictures I produced. I made half my income from Jackie pictures in 1971. *Tennis* magazine, for example, paid me $450 for that series of Jackie and Caroline at the tennis courts. And I can sell those

Mid-February, 1969: Ari stops to talk in front of the Carlyle Hotel. He asked me why I am a paparazzo, so I asked him if he'd give me a job as a photographer for Olympic airlines. "Yes," he said, "and for that I would pay you one dollar ... " Later I worked with a false mustache, hoping not to be recognized.

pictures to other publications, too. Almost every magazine in the world wants pictures of Jackie.

There are a lot of disadvantages to being a paparazzo, too, of course. You have to be a certain type of person. You have to be thick-skinned so that it doesn't bother you to have people call you names. And sometimes you have to be prepared to be beaten up, too. You have to be patient. You have to wait hours at a time for people to come out of their apartments or restaurants or theatres and that can get very cold when you're waiting during the winter, just sitting out in your car, freezing while you're waiting for Jackie and Ari to come out of El Morocco.

I'm a loner. You have to be a person who enjoys being by himself because a paparazzo doesn't have much of a social life. Most of his social life, most of his contact with the world, is through his subjects. You meet a lot of doormen with sore feet and tough chauffeurs and crazy fans and cranky Secret Servicemen, but you don't meet many beautiful girls. Not as many as you might think.

When you take out girls they have to be a special kind of girl. For instance, you might invite a girl out to a movie and

Jackie and Lee Radziwill's exit from the theatre after a performance of *Company* turned into a melee of photographers and onlookers. Jackie and Lee got a big kick out of the photographers taking pictures.

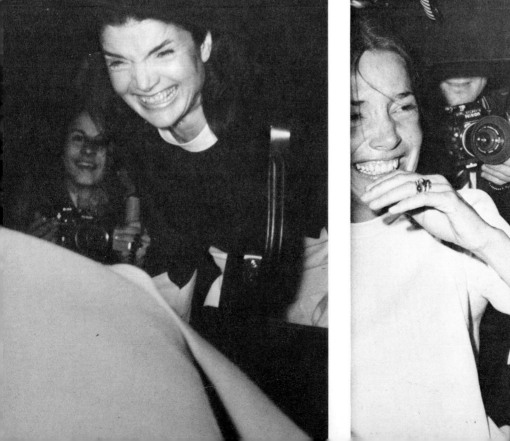

then discover that Jackie is on her way to an art gallery. And so you have to take the girl to the art gallery. Not every girl would fit in there. Also, a lot of girls don't like that.

I did take out one girl who liked to do that a lot. In fact, when I told her we'd have to go to a premiere to take pictures of celebrities, she said, "Oh, let's get my mother. She'd like to come along." And so I had to drive way out to Brooklyn to get her mother. And then it turned out that her brother wanted to come along too. So there were four of us going to shoot paparazzi.

It takes a lot of photographic equipment. When you start out to be a paparazzo you can get along with one good 35mm camera. But I have a lot more than that and you need more than that to be really good. I have three Nikon f's and two Nikon f-2's. One of them has a motor drive which lets me shoot four frames a second. That's the best when speed is important, for instance if you're trying to take pictures of Jackie when she's moving away from you.

But a motor drive makes noise and so it is no good when secrecy is important, such as when you're hiding near Jackie and you don't want her to hear you. For those kind of pictures I have Nikons without a motor drive. Then I have other Nikons with color and black-and-white film so that I don't have to stop and reload when I'm in a hurry.

Then I have a Rolli 35, which is as small as a pack of cigarettes. Right now I'm disguising that camera as a belt buckle and then I will fit it into a specially designed belt. That's very good for photographing someone like Ali McGraw, who is friendly and will talk to me, but is very nervous about anyone taking pictures of the baby. That way I can take pictures and she doesn't have to be upset.

My favorite basic lens for the Nikon is an 85mm, which lets you be very versatile. For long-distance shots it's great to have a 300mm and a 500mm lens. Both are telescopic, and you can buy an adapter which makes them twice as long. Finally, I have a Minolta Spotomatic light meter, which you can point at a window 50 yards away and measure the intensity of the light. That's a very sophisticated piece of equipment that only a paparazzo would need.

Two other pieces of equipment are very useful for a paparazzo: a skylight filter on each lens and a rubber lens hood. Both of these devices will help protect your camera if you drop it while you're on the run or if somebody takes a poke at it. The skylight filter, which costs a few dollars, may break but it will absorb the shock and protect the lens, which may cost several hundred dollars.

The rubber lens hood has a second purpose. When you're taking pictures through glass, you can peel back the rubber and put the camera lens right up against the glass. That way you don't get any reflection in the picture.

Often a paparazzo needs to conceal himself; he never wants to leap out at his subjects as Jackie testified that I did.

Was I falling in love with Jackie? Not really. She's beautiful, but I go for the Scandinavian type. The girl I'm going with now is Jodie, and she's Swedish-American.

Lord Snowden, Princess Margaret's husband, the photographer, saw me at a black-tie affair. He didn't know me but he noticed the rubber lens hood and he came up to me and said:

"My, my. I've never seen one of those. Where did you get it?"

So I told him. Maybe he wants to shoot paparazzo. You never know.

A paparazzo needs a car. A couple of years ago I bought a $3,600 carousel-red Pontiac Firebird with spoke wheels and stereo am/fm radio. You don't need a car as nice as that but it helps me look as though I belong. You fit right into the best parking lots with a car like that. The Secret Servicemen couldn't believe it the first time they saw me drive up in that car.

You need some basic disguises for some situations so celebrities don't always recognize you. I have my sunglasses, pipe, hippie wig, salt and pepper wig, Afro wig and several mustaches. I also have some special disguises for special occasions, but I'll get to them later. It helps to have a press card. I usually get one from the *Sydney Morning Herald* because I do many assignments for them; therefore I'm authorized to have one. Sometimes a press card helps because you find that you can get into places legitimately. Of course, a lot of the time you don't need credentials at all; such as in public places like hotel lobbies, airports or on the street.

I always keep my passport ready and $500 in traveler's checks because you never know when you're going to have to follow somebody off to Europe at a moment's notice. You have to have something to put all your cameras and equipment in. I never use an ordinary camera bag because that's a dead give-away that I'm a photographer. I use a duffle bag or an airline bag, or sometimes a mailbag. A mailbag serves two purposes. It hides my cameras and I can pretend that I'm a mailman. That way people don't get suspicious when, for example, I'm asking around St. Tropez how to find Brigitte Bardot's house.

A lot of people think that paparazzi have no ethics. That's not true for me. I like to catch the stars when they're looking beautiful—very natural. People ask me if I feel guilty about invading people's privacy. I don't believe I'm invading anyone's privacy. If they discover me and object to being photographed, I stop. I play it by ear. Most celebrities don't mind being paparazzied. I stay off people's property and take the pictures from a distance. I'm not like some European paparazzi who would crash right into a bedroom to take pictures.

Of course, if you should happen to live in a glass house. . . .

5

the Peapack caper

I didn't even know there was a place called Peapack until I read in the New York papers one time that John had hurt his hand while horseback riding near Peapack. I did a little investigating and found out that Peapack is a very small town about fifty miles southwest of New York in the rolling green hills of New Jersey where Jackie has rented what she calls a bungalow. Some bungalow! To me it was more like a mansion on an estate.

Friday afternoons after school the Secret Servicemen get the stationwagon out and put Caroline's and John's bicycles or sleds, depending on the season, in the back and head for Peapack. Jackie picks up John at school in the limousine and she heads for Peapack, too. A weekend in the country.

Ari doesn't go out there very often. Ari likes good restaurants and clubs like they have in New York. They don't have much in the way of good food around Peapack. I understand that Jackie and the children sometimes stop off at Howard Johnson's on the way out. That's not Ari's style.

I heard from one of the local policemen out there that there's another reason Ari doesn't like Peapack. Ari is a great walker. After dinner, even late at night, he likes to walk around New York and I think he likes to walk around Paris and London and Athens the same way. One night he tried

77

This is what Jackie calls her bungalow, in Peapack, New Jersey.

walking around Peapack. People don't usually walk in Peapack. Everybody has cars. So the cops are liable to pick you up as a suspicious character when you're walking late at night.

When he told them he was Aristotle Onassis, they thought he had escaped from a nearby asylum. This is true. One of the cops told me this. Ari doesn't look like a billionaire when you see him. He dresses very plainly. He's Old World, like my father. He likes good food and good wine, but he doesn't care anything about clothes. So the police took Ari down to the station house until the Secret Service came down and identified him.

Peapack is not Ari's style. I sympathize with him. I had a similar experience in Peapack myself. I was sleeping in my car

The Secret Servicemen generally bring John and Caroline's bicycles out to Peapack for summer weekends in the country.

along the side of the highway one night and the cops came along and told me I couldn't sleep there.

Actually, though, Peapack is a friendly place and I used to look forward to those weekends in the country until the Secret Service fixed it so I couldn't go back anymore. That's what I call my Peapack caper.

My adventures in Peapack started slowly. On my first trip the people in the town were cooperative and they told me where the bungalow was, up a road that was lined with a beautiful colonnade of trees and flowers. But on the first couple of trips up there I didn't even see Jackie. She doesn't go out very much in Peapack. Once I tried to follow her on a fox hunt but my car got stuck in the mud. I got a picture of John on his bicycle on one trip but it wasn't until after

After a few trips I finally got this picture of Jackie. I sold
it to several publications—even her back is famous!

several trips that I finally caught sight of Jackie walking
down the road.

But she must have seen my car and known it was me
because she didn't even turn around. I had to be satisfied
with a picture of her back. But I sold that picture to several
publications! That shows that Jackie is so popular that even a
picture of her back can be sold.

There was one day that Jackie did cooperate. I think she
cooperated better on that day than ever before or since. I had
a hunch that Jackie was going to be at the St. Bernard's
Horse Show in Gladstone, near Peapack, and so I planned to
be there myself. I figured I would disguise myself to fit
inconspicuously into the crowd and so I put on my blue jeans
and a sports shirt and my sunglasses and a souvenir hat that I

had picked up the year before at the Chuck Connors Golf Tournament in Palm Springs. The hat said "Chuck Connors International" right on it. For some reason it also had a picture of a horse, and so I figured that I'd look like an official and fit right in. But I wasn't as inconspicuous as I hoped. Well, how was I to know that Jackie and everybody else was going to be wearing jodhpurs and riding hats? I had never been to a horse show before. I stood out in the crowd and the Secret Service spotted me instantly. Walsh came over, but for once was very calm.

"Hello," he said politely. He introduced me to another agent, Mike Dolphin.

"Look," I said. "Let's not have another incident. I don't want to get close. I'll just use the long lens."

Walsh thought it over for a minute and then he walked over and conferred with Jackie. They talked for a few minutes and Walsh came back.

"Let Mr. Galella take as many pictures as he wants," Walsh told Dolphin. And so I did. Jackie was smiling all afternoon and although I didn't get any pictures of her riding, I got pictures of Caroline and John riding and John winning a medal.

They were so cooperative, I suppose, because it was a public place, definitely, and there was no reason not to

I thought I'd fit right in at the St. Bernard's Horse Show in my blue jeans and golf hat. My mistake.

Jackie, John-John, and Caroline at St. Bernard's School
Seventeenth Annual Horse Show.

cooperate. There was even another photographer there, a photographer from one of the local papers. But that guy didn't know what he was doing. He took pictures of all the winners—whether they were Kennedys or not! Well, maybe that's what *his* papers wanted. He had his job and I had mine and for once we all got what we wanted that afternoon. It was very friendly. I will always remember it as the only completely pleasant afternoon that I have ever spent photographing Jackie.

Certainly, it was very different from the afternoon when the trouble began. That was a Saturday afternoon in the summer and Tom Wargacki and I had gone down to Peapack together. When we were down there I found out that Jackie and the children had gone out on a picnic. "Oh, great," I thought, "a picnic will make a terrific picture."

My problem was how to get close enough to them without being spotted by the Secret Service agents who would be watching from a high vantage point near the bungalow. And so I asked one of the neighborhood kids to come along with me. I carried his fishing pole over my shoulder, and so we looked like a father and son going fishing. From a distance my camera bag looked like a fishing bag.

For once the Secret Service agents were very calm and cooperative. It was the only completely pleasant afternoon I ever spent photographing Jackie.

It worked pretty well. I got some beautiful long distance pictures of Jackie lying down watching Caroline doing handstands. Unfortunately, I got there late and only had a chance to take a couple of pictures before they packed up and walked across the field and climbed over the fence to go home. It was a very peaceful scene, very nice, with Jackie and the children together. I've said it before and I'll say it again: I think Jackie tries to be a very good mother. She's very close to the children. People ask me why I don't feel guilty about intruding on a private, domestic scene like that. I don't feel guilty because they didn't know I was there. If they knew I was there, and I broke it up, then I would feel guilty.

But that wasn't the end of the day. Later almost toward evening, I saw Jackie get into the station wagon with John

With one of the neighborhood kids along with me, from a distance I looked like a fisherman.

and a friend of John's. One of the rich McDonnell boys. Jackie was driving. That was very unusual for Jackie to be driving. Usually the Secret Service or the chauffeur drives. I wanted a picture of that and so Tom Wargacki and I followed. Jackie drove into Peapack and stopped the station wagon across the street from the drugstore and went inside.

Tom stayed in the car waiting to get a picture of her when she came out, but I had another plan. I went to the window of the drugstore and saw Jackie looking at the magazine rack only about five feet away. I had never been so close to her before without her noticing me. And so I put the lens up against the window and started taking pictures. Incidentally, if you are taking pictures through a tinted glass, like the windows on some cars, open the shutter one more stop than

It was a very peaceful scene, very nice, with Jackie and the children together. I think Jackie tries to be a very good mother.

Unfortunately I got there late and only got the chance to take a few pictures before they climbed the fence to go home.

People ask me why I don't feel guilty about intruding on a private scene like this; if I broke it up, then I would feel guilty.

you would ordinarily to allow for the dimming of the light. For example, if you would be shooting f8, set it at f5.6 instead. I made this allowance, although the window was not tinted, but was dirty.

And then I saw the shot that I knew I had to have. Jackie was standing at the counter with John and his friend in bare feet and she was paying for her magazines and their ice cream. It wasn't like Bonwit Teller's, where she just said, "Send them." She was paying for them with real money, just like any ordinary American woman. Stop to think how rare it is for Jackie to have to soil her hands with money and you'll realize why I had to have the picture. Magazines and news-papers are crazy about shots like that. I simply had to have it. But to get it I had to stand in the doorway. She saw me and I could see that she was getting mad. She went over to one of the owners, and I knew she would throw me out if I stayed. So I walked away. That's a good rule for a paparazzo. Walk away in a situation like that. Don't run. You might trip and break a camera.

But when Jackie came out and got into her car, I got some pictures of her again. That did it. She really got mad. She started to beep her horn. Beep! Beep! Beep! That's what Jackie calls communicating. Beep! Beep! Beep! But I got the message. She was saying that she wasn't going to leave until I left first. She didn't want to be followed to the Murray McDonnell horse farm. Beep! Beep! I got the message and left.

Things still didn't seem too bad so far. Tom and I ran into the Secret Service agents at a diner that night and they were friendly, and so I guess that Jackie hadn't told them about the drugstore incident—at least not yet.

The next day was Sunday and I wanted to get some pictures of Jackie going to church. Now I knew that there were three Catholic churches in the area that she might be going to, but I didn't know which one. What I did was this. I followed her car from the bungalow and as soon as I could tell which church she was going to, I took a shortcut and got to the church before her and the Secret Service.

When they pulled up, in front of the church, I saw Walsh was surprised—and angry—that Tom and I had beaten them. They were so mad that they blocked our way so we couldn't get any pictures of her going into or out of the church.

Would I take pictures of her in the church? I would not, unless the light was good and I could do it without anybody noticing me. But I knew in that little church I was going to

Jackie buying magazines and ice cream with real money, just like any ordinary American woman.

90

be noticed. And there was no chance of taking pictures through the window, because I hadn't figured out yet how to photograph through stained glass. So that time they had me. But they weren't willing to let it go at that. No, they really wanted to get even.

After church Walsh had a long talk with Jackie. I guess she told him everything because he came over to my car, puffed up and red, as if he had something important on his mind.

"Now you've done it," Walsh said and he unbuttoned his jacket so I could see he was carrying a gun in a shoulder holster. "This time you've really done it. Now she's busting my balls."

Walsh was staring at me, angry, but I didn't look at him at all.

"I'm going to have to take you in." he said. "For trespassing."

One of the other agents got into my car and Walsh climbed into a Secret Service car and we all drove off to the Peapack police station. I was nervous when we got there, but I knew that I had a secret weapon and I was prepared to use it. The police had already made out my summons and Walsh had handed it to me when I made my move.

"Walsh," I said, "if you go through with this, you know what I'm going to do? I'm going to have a *hundred* paparazzi out here. And not only that, I'm going to tell them the whole layout."

I could tell right away that Walsh got my message. I knew that he was impressed with my familiarity with the neighborhood. When we got to the church before he did, he told me that I knew the area better than he did. I knew what was going through his mind. He was thinking of hundreds of paparazzi, pressing their lenses against the drugstore window, running in front of the church, walking behind Jackie with fishing poles and camera bags. I could see what was going through his mind. He was thinking hard.

He took back the summons from me. Without a word he pulled a pen and started writing something on a plain piece of paper. Then he handed me the paper and I read it:

"I Ron Galella, promise that I will never take pictures of the Kennedys in Peapack again."

Walsh wanted me to sign it. He was offering me a compromise: No trespassing charges, if I promised never to take pictures in Peapack again.

"Sign it," Walsh said.

I signed it and gave it back to him. Walsh put the paper in his pocket. That was it. The great Peapack Compromise. As Tom and I drove away headed back for New York, I was a little sad to think that I would never be able to take pictures in Peapack again.

Jackie, looking at magazines in the drugstore in Peapack.

6

summer in Skorpios

I skipped the wedding.

Actually, I was in Paris when I heard that Jackie and Ari were going to get married and I even thought about grabbing a plane over. But I was tired, really exhausted. I had spent a month trying to do a paparazzo job on Liz Taylor who was in Paris making *The Only Game in Town* with Warren Beatty. Liz can be very difficult, as difficult as Jackie when she wants to be, and by the time I got the pictures I needed for a *Cosmopolitan* cover and inside spread, I was physically and mentally worn out. When I heard that in Skorpios they were throwing photographers into the water, that's all I needed to know. I decided that I wasn't up to that trip and I caught a plane back to New York.

It wasn't until the following summer that I decided that Skorpios was worth it and I made my plans. What encouraged me was a cover and spread of Jackie in a bikini that had appeared in *Life.* Those pictures had been taken by a Greek photographer, Dmitrios Koulouris, and I knew that if he could do it, so could I. It was risky, flying to Greece, of course, because Jackie might just decide to come back to New York or spend the summer in some other place, and I'd be stuck there in Greece with nothing to take pictures of but statues. But I decided to take the chance and on July 15th

1970 with $1,500 in travelers checks, my cameras, 50 rolls of film and a few clothes I flew non-stop from New York to Athens.

Right away I discovered that I should have done more research, because when I arrived in Athens I remembered that I didn't know where Skorpios was, and there weren't many Greeks who knew either. And so I killed a few days in Athens, partly for fun and partly to get my bearings. I went to some fashion shows and sneaked into the pool at the Hilton. That's a pushover for a paparazzo. By the way I always try to stay near a Hilton Hotel when I'm abroad. That way I stay up–to–date on the latest information. The Greek newspapers, even if I could read them, are always a few days behind the news.

Little by little, I started to put together my information. The people at Olympic Airlines were very helpful. If Ari only knew. They gave me the name of an artist in Athens from whom Jackie had bought some paintings. And they pointed out to me Ari's house in the suburb of Glafada, where Jackie and Ari sometimes spend a night or two when they're in Athens. I staked it out for a day but I didn't see any sign of them. The Associated Press bureau in Athens confirmed that Jackie and Ari were still on Skorpios.

In the meantime I had found out where Scorpios is. With the help of a map and a Greek guy who had a wife from Boston I learned that Skorpios was about 175 miles north-northwest of Athens. To get there I would have to take an Olympic flight to the town of Aktion and from there I would have to take a taxi to the tiny fishing village of Nydri, which would have to be my headquarters. I couldn't go any farther than that—a mile and a half off the coast—there was Skorpios, and on Skorpios there was no friendly face, no clean bed, no fish and wine for me.

The Greek with the wife from Boston wrote down some useful phrases that I could use with the fishermen of Nydri, like, "How much do you charge to take me around Skorpios?" But even so I was nervous. I had to fly Ari's airline and survive in Ari's land, and you hear some bad things about the Greek government. As a precaution I got a Greek press card and I also signed the register at the U.S. Embassy. If I was going to be missing in action, I wanted the world to know where I disappeared from.

The plane ride to Aktion was fine. Maybe the crew knew that I was a paparazzo going to take pictures of their boss and his wife, but if they did, it didn't seem to bother them. The taxi ride out of Aktion was long and hot and the taxi stirred up big clouds of white limestone dust, but Spiros, the driver, was friendly and as soon as we got to Nydri he took me right up to Dmitrios Koulouris, who was playing handball with a friend. When he found out who I was he was happy to

Greek artist Skalido is shown here with a painting of his similar to one bought by Jackie for her New York apartment.

Here's one of Ari's airplanes flying over Ari's sister's house on Skorpios.

see me. Because he didn't understand any English, I congratulated him on his bikini pictures in Italian. Then Spiros made a terrible mistake. To Spiros I suppose it was the natural thing to do. He led me through town, right to this little cafe on the beach and right up to the only people in town who could speak English—two Secret Service agents! One of them was Mike Dolphin and he looked at me, trying to remember.

"You are the guy from Peapack, aren't you?" Dolphin said at last. "You've lost weight."

That was it. He didn't seem mad or tell me to get lost, or ask me what I was doing there. He knew what I was doing there. Maybe he was even happy to have me around as a kind of diversion. There were five agents who were assigned to watch John and Caroline on Skorpios and when they weren't on duty all they had to do was go swimming or wait their turn to go to Athens. It must have been boring, and maybe Dolphin figured that with me there would be some action.

"Yeah," I said. "I've lost weight. I've been running around a lot."

There are only 500 people in Nydri and only two hotels, and as only one of the hotels was clean enough to stay in, the agents and I saw a lot of each other. We even shared the same shower room. Chief agent Walsh must have been off on his rest period in Athens when I arrived, but in a couple of days he was back in Nydri (probably notified that I was there), keeping his eye on me a lot of the time. And I knew that as soon as Walsh knew, he had given the news to Jackie: Galella-baby is here. Still I felt pretty silly about all my fears and suspicions about coming here.

In the meantime, I had been doing some intelligence work of my own. The first night I arrived I made contact with the fishermen and it was wonderful to learn that they were happy to see me. They love paparazzi! They talk, with longing, about the time Jackie and Ari got married and how many paparazzi came and how good business was then. Some of them even knew English and I made an agreement with a guy named Johnny to take me out the next day. There are definite police rules about going around Skorpios. Tourists with no cameras are allowed to go as close as 100 meters to the shore, but paparazzi have to stay 300 meters off shore. I didn't like that and so we found a policeman who was watching a card game, and Johnny asked him if I could go tourist. Sure, he said. See, you can't always believe what you hear. The Greek police were nice to me, nicer by far than the U.S. Secret Service.

The next day I paid Johnny 300 drachmas (about five dollars) and he took me on my first reconnaissance tour of Skorpios. I could see right away that it was like an independent country, a very self-sufficient island with its own gardens and animals. I took a few pictures of the island itself on that first trip, but I didn't even catch sight of Jackie.

Nights I spent at the cafe in Nydri, talking to the fishermen and Dmitirios and to the sailors from the *Christina* who

On my first trip I photographed one of the Onassis' homes, but I didn't even catch sight of Jackie.

July and August, 1970. Skorpios is heavily guarded with Greek police, sailors from the *Christina* and the Secret Service agents, so I disguised myself as a Greek sailor.

used to come into the village to drink ouzo and who like to talk a little about what Jackie and Ari are up to. One night I learned that they planned to fly out early in the seaplane the next day to have a picnic with some friends on another island.

Oh great, I thought. I'll get pictures of them coming back to Skorpios after the picnic. And so the next afternoon Johnny took me out and sure enough there was the seaplane coming in about half a mile away. But something else was coming too, speeding across the water towards us. It was the Secret Service boat with Walsh and another U.S. agent, a Greek American named James Kalafatis.

"You," said Walsh as they pulled up alongside us, "You are interfering with the landing of a seaplane."

That was a surprise charge but it was no joke. Demitrios later got six months in jail on that same charge.

"We're not interfering anymore than you are," I told Walsh. "We're nowhere near the seaplane."

"Who did you pay off to find out about this?" Walsh said.

"No one," I said. "You know something? This is Greece where democracy got started. And what you're doing is undemocratic."

"Oh yeah?" said Walsh. "Ask Kalafatis about Greek democracy."

They both laughed. There wasn't much we could do after that. Johnny and I exchanged a few more words, but the agents really won that round. We had to go back to Nydri.

I was not running in luck. Every day I came out and there were times when I got good pictures. I had a nice take of John and Caroline and the Radziwill children playing on John's boat, but I couldn't get any good pictures of Jackie. I was getting impatient.

I looked forward to Jackie's forty-first birthday on July 28th. There'll be a big party, I thought, and I'll get some terrific stuff. I wasn't the only one who thought so. The day before Jackie's birthday who should show up in Nydri but two other paparazzi—Tom Wargacki from New York and

Secret Service agents in the Chris-Craft at the left prevented me from photographing the landing of Jackie's seaplane. Below, agent John Walsh sits toward the stern. Agent James Kalafatis sits beside him, his hand over the water.

John Howard, an Australian. I was happy to see them and that night we had a talk at the cafe and even Walsh sat down with us. He didn't say anything to me or Tom but he was friendly with Howard. That puzzled me. Why was a Secret Service agent friendly to a paparazzo?

The next day, Tom and Howard and I cruised around the island and got some pictures of John alone in the little red and white speed boat that Ari had given him. He drives it very well. But still no Jackie. That night when we got back to Nydri we found out that we had missed what would have been a good take. After we left him, John had given Jackie a ride and they drove to within 50 yards of the shore at Nydri. If we had only stayed in Nydri, we would have gotten the pictures.

Tom and John left in a few days, disappointed. But I stayed. I knew what had to be done now. There was no other way. I had put it off long enough. I had to try a landing on Skorpios itself. On a boat trip around the island you were only in front of the beach for a few minutes and the chances of Jackie showing up and swimming or playing with a beach ball or doing anything at just the right minute were not good.

No, I had to try the landing, set up my equipment on the

John-John, Caroline and their cousin Tony Radziwill go for a spin in John's boat. I took these pictures from another boat, wearing my sailor disguise.

Here the children are with their governess. The boat was
a present from Ari; John, who was nine when I took
these pictures, drives it as fast as he likes.

shore and wait for her. It was risky, but I knew it could be done. Dmitrios had done it—so could I. That night I found another fisherman, one who was willing to land me on Skorpios. His name was Zios and he had one disadvantage: he couldn't speak one word of English. But I handed him a map and some drawings and showed him what I wanted. The next day Zios picked me up at 9 a.m. I was wearing a bathing suit, sailor hat, polo shirt, and shower clogs and carried a rain coat to protect myself from the brambles. I dressed very casually because I wasn't going to any dance or party. Along with my cameras I carried a few peaches, a candy bar and a bottle of water, all in a small duffel bag.

Zios put me down in the hold where the motor emitted exhaust fumes. It was hot and the exhaust kept drifting in, but Zios didn't want to take the chance of the police seeing me so he put a blanket over me. An hour later we reached the island and Zios put me on shore on a little peninsula with a lot of trees and bushes. For ten minutes I crawled through the bushes until I came to the other side of the peninsula. Through the branches I could look out across a little bay and, a couple of hundred meters away, there was the beach and the beach house.

An afternoon on Skorpios. I hid under a tree for hours to get these pictures.

There were about 150 people working on the island, including the *Christina* sailors. I don't know what they would have done if they had found me. I don't think they would have put me in jail. Ari and I had not been too unfriendly up to then. He might even have welcomed me. The thing that really bothered me most was snakes, but anyhow I made myself a nest under a tree and waited.

At 11 a.m. I saw two sailors appear and they hosed down the patio and everything. Getting ready for the queen, I thought. And then a woman in a bikini came down to the shore and started doing exercises. But it wasn't Queen Jackie. It was the Princess—Lee Radziwill. Lee looked very good doing her Yoga. Then Jackie came down, wearing pink Levis. Good, I thought, she'll join in. But Jackie just watched. A little later I got pictures of Caroline water-skiing. But still no action shots of Jackie. It was getting late and I had to rendezvous with Zios and so I climbed out of my nest and left.

The next day we came out again, but things went badly. It took Zios 45 minutes to get the engine started and the exhaust was worse than ever. Jackie would have laughed if she could have seen me lying there in the bottom of the boat,

I don't think the people working on the island would have put me in jail if they'd found me; mostly I was worried about snakes.

Zios, the real Greek sailor, by Ron Galella; Ron Galella, the imitation Greek sailor, by Zios.

choking. Nobody came to the beach that day and so the only picture I got was one of myself, which I took by setting the timer on the camera and then running around in front of it. This was something like the time I was in the Air Force, although I was never a pilot myself. But they had to take pictures of the target area just to prove they'd been there.

The situation got even worse. The next day I heard that Jackie was going back to the States. I had to follow her, at least as far as Athens. But I was getting more frustrated. About $500 worth of travelers checks had disappeared, and by the time I got to Athens airport Jackie had already gotten out of the helicopter and into the plane for New York. I got pictures of the children but not of Jackie. But I knew she would be coming back to Skorpios. And so would I.

Well, Jackie needed a change for a while, and I did too. My agent in New York had told me that Liz Taylor and Richard Burton were going to be docking at Le Havre in the Queen Elizabeth II early in August, and so from Athens I flew off to Paris, where I met with an old friend, French paparazzo Henri Pessar. Henri's wife drove us to Le Havre and we were in plenty of time to get some good pictures of Liz and Richard coming off the ship. We decided to follow them to

SKORPIOS

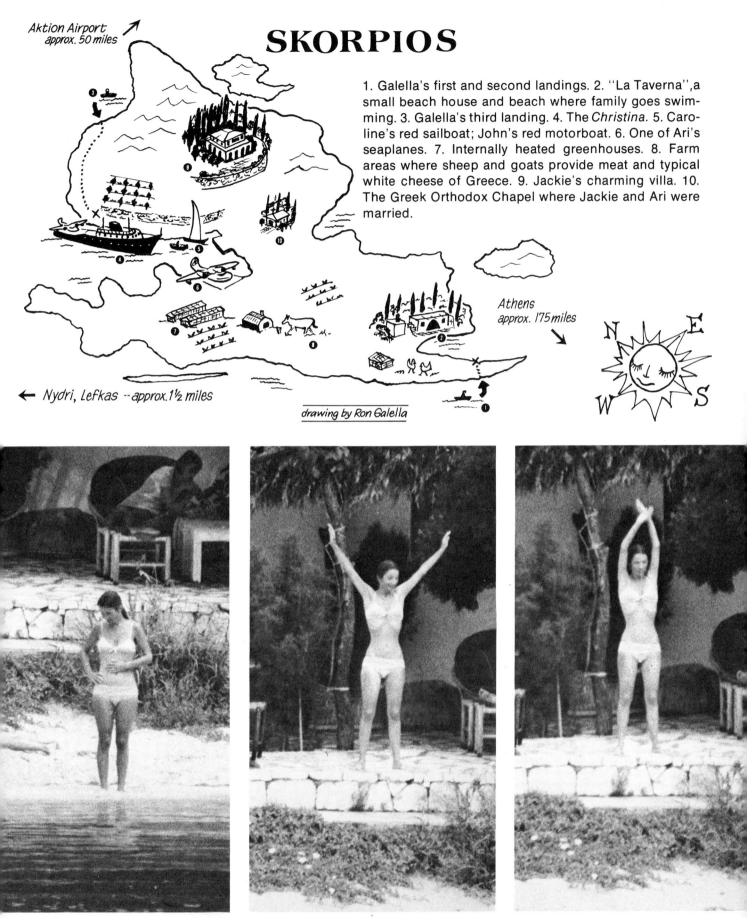

Aktion Airport
approx. 50 miles

1. Galella's first and second landings. 2. "La Taverna", a small beach house and beach where family goes swimming. 3. Galella's third landing. 4. The *Christina*. 5. Caroline's red sailboat; John's red motorboat. 6. One of Ari's seaplanes. 7. Internally heated greenhouses. 8. Farm areas where sheep and goats provide meat and typical white cheese of Greece. 9. Jackie's charming villa. 10. The Greek Orthodox Chapel where Jackie and Ari were married.

Athens
approx. 175 miles

← Nydri, Lefkas --approx. 1½ miles

drawing by Ron Galella

Lee Radziwill looked good doing her yoga exercises; I hoped Jackie would join her, but no luck.

105

Deauville, and that's where Burton, upon leaving an Italian restaurant, looked at me, and said in that great Shakespearean voice:

"If you intend to follow me to the south of France I shall have to be constrained to keep from killing you."

On that note, we left. Back we went to Paris. I thought Burton was kidding about going to the south of France but that's where he went. I caught up with them and took pictures of Liz and Richard boarding their yacht at Monte Carlo, from a safe distance of course. If Burton wasn't kidding about going to the south of France, maybe he wasn't kidding about killing me either. But I was getting restless, restless for Jackie.

I flew back to Athens and then to Aktion. This time I took the bus to Nydri and it was even hotter and longer and dustier than the cab, but the bus driver let me ride free because he saw my mailbag which I use for my camera equipment and thought I was the mailman. Just one of those breaks that everyone, even a paparazzo, gets once in a while. I got back to Nydri just in time because Marguerite—she was

The same afternoon I photographed Caroline out water skiing.

A self-portrait on Skorpios, after a hand-over-hand climb up a fifty-foot cliff—the price of success.

a friendly and pretty medical student who was spending the summer with relatives in Nydri—told me Jackie and Ari were going to leave on the *Christina* the next day for their annual Mediterranean cruise. That didn't give me much time. And so that afternoon I made another reconnaissance tour from the fishing boat and I saw what I had to do next.

The next morning I told Zios to drop me off at a spot very close to the *Christina,* so near that I knew there would be a lot of people around. But I had one thing going for me. No Secret Service. John and Caroline had already left Skorpios to spend the rest of the summer in Hyannisport and the agents had gone with them. That meant all I had to worry about was Ari's 150 sailors, chauffeurs, gardeners, carpenters, waiters, cooks and maids. And the Greek police.

The ground was very rough where Zios left me off. I had to climb up a fifty foot cliff. When I got to the top after pulling myself up hand–over–hand like a commando, it was worse, but in a different way. It was *too* smooth, too civilized, too cultivated. There were no rough brambles and wild trees to hide in. I could be seen too easily. Finally, I found some skimpy bushes and hid in them.

And then I saw her. Jackie! She was down in the water swimming with her bathing cap on and her sunglasses. She didn't even know I was there and she was wearing sunglasses right in the water! But she was close, so close that I could hear Ari calling to her:

"Don't come over hee-ahh. The water is duurrrty."

It was the closest I had been to her so far on that trip. And after taking pictures of Jackie I got some of Ari up on the *Christina* and then some other shots of the two of them getting into a jeep and going away from the *Christina*.

Then suddenly I felt this spray of water on me like a shower, and I looked up. This old woman was standing there in this black peasant costume and she was holding a hose. An old crone watering Ari's gardens. I had been found out. What was she going to do? Scream? Hit me with something? I put my finger to my lips asking her to be quiet. She giggled. She looked at my camera. She laughed. She just kept laughing and watering until it was time for her to go.

In all the spraying I hadn't noticed whether Jackie and Ari had gotten back on the *Christina* or not. I wanted to take a picture of them departing but I couldn't wait. I had to rendezvous with Zios. I slid back down the slippery cliff. Zios picked me up, and as we were pulling away from the island a fast boat started coming our way. Zios got scared. He was afraid it was the police and that we were going to be caught

My trouble got me these pictures of Jackie taking a swim.

too close to Skorpios, and so he pushed me down to the bottom of the boat. When I got up I saw what a terrible mistake Zios had made. It wasn't the police at all. It was Jackie and Ari on their launch headed towards the *Christina.* That would have made a great departing picture, but it was too late. They were too far away from me now. That Zios! Nuts!

I had to say goodbye to Skorpios for good now and to Nydri too. I knew Jackie wouldn't be back this summer. All the way on the dusty road to Aktion I kept thinking about how something was missing. I had some good shots of the children and some good ones of Lee Radziwill exercising, but not enough of Jackie. I couldn't go back to New York. No, not quite yet. I needed something more.

From the sailors I had learned that the *Christina* would be stopping for fuel at Naples. As fast as I could, I got a flight to Athens and then to Rome and then a train to Naples, where I arrived the same day the *Christina* was supposed to dock. But I had a hunch. I knew how much Jackie loved Capri, and so instead of waiting in Naples I caught the ferry to Capri.

I was right! My luck was starting to change. Crossing the bay of Naples I got sight of the *Christina*, headed towards Capri. Things were going my way for a change. On shore in Capri I found the chauffeur who was supposed to meet them. I asked him what time the *Christina* was going to dock and he

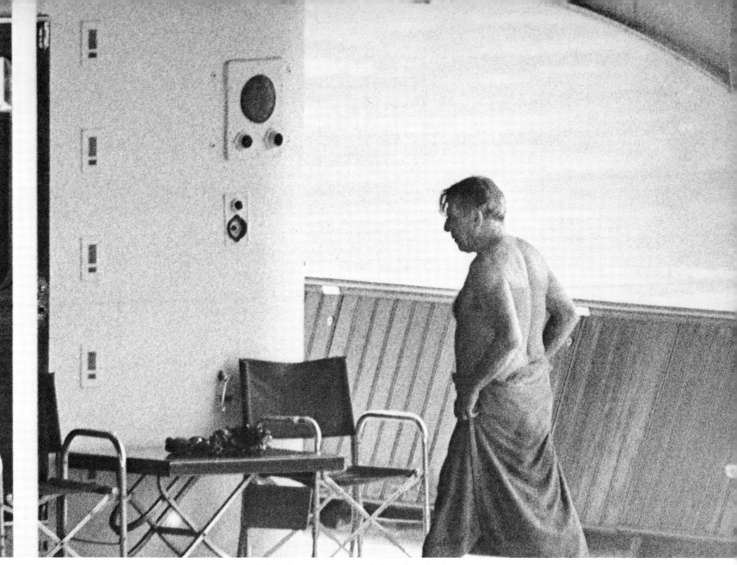

Ari relaxes aboard the *Christina.*

told me. He saw my sailor suit and must have thought I was part of the crew.

That afternoon, after they docked, I followed Jackie up to the shopping area of Capri. She saw me. It was the first time she had seen me that summer, even though she must have known from Walsh that I was hanging around Skorpios. As soon as she spotted me, Jackie turned to Lee Radziwill and said:

"Oh. There's that man again."

I followed them as they went on their shopping trip from one boutique to another. Jackie went into a jewelry store, but I didn't see her buy anything. Then she bought four pairs of sandals and then some tomato seeds for the garden on Skorpios. I was close to her, about 15-20 feet taking pictures.

Then I saw her buy some magazines, including a copy of *Gente* that had a picture of Ari and Maria Callas kissing on the cover. I think she was annoyed that I took a picture of that.

She went into an outdoor cafe where she ordered iced

August 22, 1970: The *Christina* departs for Capri. Ari is building a new yacht which will be called the *Jacqueline.*

coffee with whipped cream. Then she said something but not to me. She called over the waiter and said to him, pointing at me:

"Call the police and have them take that man away."

Let me repeat the rule. Never stay around when somebody really gets mad at you and so I left. But an hour later I came back and saw them coming out of a different cafe. This time Ari and Stas—Prince Stanislaus Radziwill, Lee's husband had joined them and Ari recognized me right away. "Come stay," he said, very friendly. We shook hands.

"What are you doing here?" Ari asked. Jackie was a few feet away and I think she was mad at Ari for talking to me. "You go all over the world?" That amazed him that a paparazzo could travel.

"Yes," I said, "I was even on Skorpios looking for you."

Then, Ari's expression got serious.

"Did you take those bikini pictures?" he asked with a frown. "I didn't like those. How would you like it if somebody took pictures of you with your pants down?"

"No, no." I said. "I didn't take those." I sympathized with Ari. We separated then. They went back to the *Christina* and I went to get some sleep.

By this time word had got around that Ari and Jackie were on Capri and some other paparazzi flew in from Rome. The *Christina* had already left Capri by the next day but fortunately two paparazzi who had come in by helicopter saw it anchored off Ischia, a nice ·resort island only a few miles away. Five of us chartered a helicopter for Ischia and then, in a fishing boat, we caught up with Ari and Jackie while they were swimming off their launch.

As soon as they saw us, of course, they got back onto the launch and sped off to the *Christina.* We all got a picture of Jackie giving somebody a kiss before she went downstairs. We all thought it was Ari, but Jackie said later in court that it was really Stas. Now that I look at the picture closely, I see that she was telling the truth. It was Stas. All of us paparazzi tried to get Jackie and Ari up on the deck again by singing "*Arrividerci, Christina.*" But it didn't work. They stayed downstairs.

Soon the *Christina* sailed off again, off to Tunisia. I

I caught up with Jackie out for a shopping expedition on Capri.

couldn't follow her there. It was too far away and my 45 day airline ticket was about to run out. But, looking back on it, it was a really good summer. Those final takes in Capri and Ischia gave me good stuff to bring back. I had worked hard for them.

Just about at the end of the action in Ischia, John Howard, the Australian paparazzo, showed up again. And I think I suddenly realized why Walsh likes him. Everybody loves a nice paparazzo who comes late and leaves early. But you can't get the good pictures that way. Getting good pictures is hard. Everything in life is hard. You have to persevere. You can only do that when you love your work the way I do so that you stay at it. That's how you survive, at anything.

August 24, 1970. Capri, Italy: In this shop Jackie bought tomato, turnip and flower seeds for her garden on Skorpios.

This was the first time all summer that Jackie saw me. "Oh. There's that man again," she said.

My sailor disguise didn't work this time. At an outdoor cafe she asked the waiter to call the police and have me arrested.

A few of us chartered a helicopter to photograph Ari and Jackie swimming off the *Christina.* We caught a picture of Jackie giving her brother-in-law a kiss just before they all went downstairs.

It doesn't take the Onassis family long to get away from you if they want to.

7

winter in New York

Greece, that is Ari's land. I'm a foreigner there. But New York is different. With all of its problems, New York is where I feel good, where I belong, where I feel sure of myself. In New York I don't have to depend on fishermen who speak strange languages. I have family and friends in New York. It's home. I have roots. I even have a business in New York. And that's how the Santa Claus episode got started.

It helps, if you're a paparazzo, to have a sideline, to have something to keep you going, particularly in the wintertime when the stars don't go out as much because of the cold. And so before Christmas every year I set up this little Santa Claus concession in a shopping center in Wayne and Little Falls, New Jersey, about 25 miles out of New York City. I built a Santa Claus house and I bought a Santa Claus uniform. The red velvet suit cost me $200 and I spent another $100 for a goat hair beard. It's a very nice outfit. And then every year I hire a Santa Claus so that the mothers can bring their children to sit on Santa's lap, and I take pictures of them.

Pictures are usually three for $5, but I send my special customers a card telling them to bring the card along with them and they can get an extra picture free. I sent one to Jackie, inviting her to bring Caroline and John out to the shopping center to have their pictures taken with Santa. She

It was good for a paparazzo to have a sideline, and this was mine.

never answered. As it happened, Jimmy Lynch, the photo editor of the *National Enquirer,* had called me up and asked me if I had any pictures of Jackie and Santa or the children and Santa. He said it would make a fine feature and I thought so too.

My Santa Claus was a guy named Patsy Greco, who used to own a bar and a restaurant in Queens and then retired. Patsy was about 74 and he had a real fat belly and he was humorous and jolly, a very good Santa Claus. I used to pay him $2 an hour to sit and have kids climb up on his lap to have their pictures taken. And so when I told him we were going to go find Jackie and have his picture taken with her, he said, "Sure. Okay. Ho. Ho. Ho."

I knew at the start that it was a difficult assignment because there was one very big advantage for Jackie! She is lean and fast and Santa is slow and fat. I put Santa in the car and off we went to New York.

The first mistake was mine. Santa and I stood right outside

Jackie's apartment in plain view of everybody. And the first time I saw Ari come up to the building I waved to him and said, "Meet Santa Claus." But Ari was in no mood for that. He just shrugged and said, "What for?" Maybe Ari was right. He could be the one man in the world who doesn't have to meet Santa Claus. He walked right by Santa without saying anything and right into the building. Worse than that he must have tipped off Jackie. He must have told her:

"Watch it. Galella's downstairs with Santa Claus."

For two days we waited outside the building without seeing Jackie come down. I was getting worried. I was paying Santa $2 an hour and we weren't getting anywhere. And not only that, I knew that Christmas was getting nearer and nearer and I had to get the pictures fast. Nobody was going to pay for pictures of Santa and Jackie in August. It had to be now.

Then, on the night of December 17th, Santa and I got our break. It was a cold night and we were waiting across the street in my car, sitting there and trying to keep warm. We weren't talking much. It's not like being with another paparazzo when there's a lot to talk about. Santa knows what he's got to do and that's it. There's not much more to talk about.

As we were sitting there, I noticed a limousine pull up and stop in front of Jackie's building. I recognized the limousine as Andre Meyer's.

"This could be it," I told Santa.

As it turned out, I was right. In a little while Jackie and Andre Meyer came down alone and got into the limousine. I guess that Ari had already left town. Andre Meyer's limousine drove down Fifth Avenue and I followed it. When they finally made a turn I was pretty sure I knew where they were going, and sure enough they pulled up in front of "21" and I stopped behind them. Santa couldn't move fast enough, and by the time he got out of the car they were already inside.

There was nothing for us to do but wait. And while we were waiting I went up to Andre Meyer's chauffeur. I gave him $10 and he told me that they were going to leave "21" pretty soon to go to the Biltmore Theatre to see *Hair.* That was $10 I was glad I spent because it gave me the information I needed to keep up with Jackie. Fast information was going to be important to make up for a slow-moving Santa.

Sure enough, after about 45 minutes, she and Andre came out of "21." But they were very clever. Jackie won that round. She had a guy from the restaurant come out before her and stand in front of Santa so I couldn't get a picture of her and Santa together. That guy stepped right on Santa's toe.

Well, Jackie may have won that one, but she didn't get away from us. She must have figured that the guy from the restaurant would hold Santa up long enough to give her a

It was a mistake to stand out in front of the Onassis apartment in plain view of everybody.

chance to get away, but what she didn't know was that Santa and I knew where she was going next. We didn't have to follow the car.

She must have been surprised when Santa and I showed up in the lobby of the Biltmore Theatre just as she and Andre were picking up their tickets. She didn't get angry, though, she just looked at Santa and then turned to Andre and said:

"He's fat!"

Sure he's fat. He's Santa Claus. During intermission I decided to leave Santa in the lobby because I didn't want to cause too much commotion inside, and I went into the theatre and took some pictures of Jackie and Andre sitting and talking in their seats. You know, Jackie seems to complain about me bothering her and her friends all the time, but I don't think her friends always mind. Long afterwards, when he saw those pictures of him and Jackie in *Life,* Andre called *Life* to get my phone number. Then his secretary called me up and ordered six prints of one of the pictures showing him.

Even so, I still didn't have a very good picture of Jackie and Santa, and so Santa and I raced back to Jackie's apartment after *Hair* was over. I finally got some pictures of Santa and Jackie together as Jackie was going into her apartment.

"Boy, you're fast," Andre said to me outside the apartment. Sure. With a speedy Jackie and a slow Santa, you have to be fast.

Santa gets his toe stepped on as Jackie and Andre Meyer leave "21."

122

My next problem was to get some pictures of Santa and the children, and so the next morning Santa and I were waiting outside Jackie's apartment again. Caroline came out and was walking the dogs. I followed her through the park. Caroline didn't mind at all. In court Jackie tried to make me look like a child molester, who was frightening the children all the time. But that's not true. I never frightened them. On this particular morning Caroline was pretty friendly. I knew that they would probably be going to England to spend Christmas with Lee and Stas Radziwill and so I asked her:

"Caroline, are you leaving for London soon?"

"Yes," she said. "Very soon."

And when Santa called out to her and said, "Merry Christmas," Caroline was very polite and answered, "Good morning."

Caroline went back inside with the dogs, but Santa and I waited and soon out came Jackie and Caroline again. They went to school, where John was singing in the Christmas choir. I watched Jackie and Caroline go inside and then I went to Kalafatis, the Secret Service agent, and asked him to let me take a few pictures of them as they were coming out. That way I wouldn't have to photograph them out at the airport when they got ready to leave for London.

"Sure," said Kalafatis. "They'll be coming right down this way."

We caught up with them as they picked up their tickets for *Hair*. All she had to say about Santa was, "He's fat."

The next morning I followed Caroline through the park. She didn't mind, and she was very polite with Santa Claus.

But they didn't. Jackie double-crossed me. She came down another way and I still missed getting good pictures of the children with Santa. The limousine took them over to Broadway and 79th Street, where they got out of the car and bought some frozen custard cones. This time I managed to take a couple of pictures of them eating ice cream cones. Then I decided I would leave them and not photograph them out at the airport. Actually, I would have liked to follow them all the way to London, but I had my Santa Claus concession to think about and Santa and I had already

Santa couldn't keep up with Jackie. She lost him, and I stayed with them until they bought ice cream cones at 79th Street and Broadway.

neglected it for too long to photograph Jackie. Goodbye Jackie. Hello, Wayne, New Jersey.

So that was the end of Jackie and Santa, except for the famous Christmas card incident, but I'll get to that later.

It wasn't the end of the winter, though, and I wanted to get some good winter scenes of Jackie and the children. I got my chance a couple of weeks after Christmas. It was a bright, cold Sunday with snow on the ground, and I had a hunch that Jackie and the children would be back from London. I figured that they would look out of the window of their apartment and see how beautiful Central Park was covered with snow and they would want to go out and walk around.

They did better than that! Caroline and John came down with sleds and went to a hill in the Park just south of the Metropolitan Museum of Art. "This is great," I thought. "Nobody has ever seen pictures of Caroline and John sledding before." Now, snow has one big disadvantage for a paparazzo. It's cold to stand in and even colder to lie down and hide in. But this time I was lucky. I didn't have to hide. Nobody bothered me. There were three Secret Service agents with the kids, but they let me stand at a distance and take my pictures. I have to hand it to the agents. They were very human that day. Maybe the Christmas spirit was still with them.

I only had one bad moment. I was standing in front of a tree at the bottom of the hill taking pictures of John when I noticed he was heading right for me.

"Oh. Oh," I said to myself, "If I jump out of the way, he's going to crash into that tree and the Secret Service is going to blame the whole thing on me."

So I did the only thing I could do. I shut my eyes and stood there waiting for John to hit me. Paparazzi are softer than trees, I thought. He won't hurt himself. But he fooled me. He swerved out of the way just in time. I should have remembered from seeing him handle that boat in Skorpios that he's a good driver.

For about two hours I took pictures of the children sledding and building snowmen. All the time, of course, they knew I was there. But it didn't bother them. Caroline even spoke to me.

"Do you like London better than New York?" I asked her as she pulled her sled past me.

"No," she said. "New York is better."

But then Jackie showed up. I guess she had been taking a walk around the reservoir and when she saw me taking pictures of her and Caroline, things started to get a little nasty then. Jackie had pulled the collar on her turtleneck sweater way up and had put on her sunglasses so that I could barely see her face. And one of the agents, Tom Tully, gave me a bump into a snowbank when he ran at me.

Jackie, Jackie, why do you do these things to me? That's what I thought then. But I learned later that there were tougher winters to come.

126

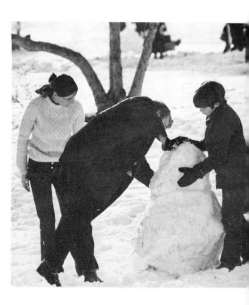

Winter wasn't over yet. A couple of weeks after Christmas, I got a hunch that Jackie and the children would be back from London, so I waited for them in Central Park on this bright, snowy Sunday. The three Secret Service agents let me stand at a distance and take my pictures; maybe the Christmas spirit was still with them.

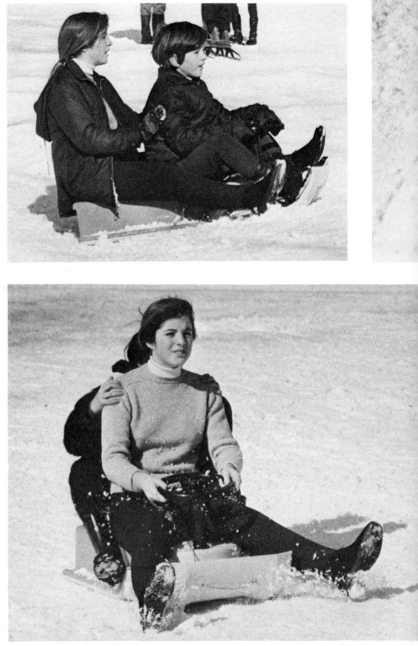

My only bad moment that day came when I noticed that John was headed right for me on his sled. "If I jump out of the way," I said to myself, "he's going to crash into that tree and the Secret Service is going to blame the whole thing on me." But he swerved out of the way just in time; he's a good driver.

128

I took pictures for about two hours; of course the children knew I was there, but they weren't bothered. But then Jackie showed up and things started to get a little nasty. One of the agents bumped me into a snowbank—but I learned later that there were tougher winters to come.

8

the Kennedy clan

Jackie is so glamorous that she almost makes you forget that the rest of the Kennedy family is exciting, too. It's a mistake to forget it because women like Ethel and Rose and Joan are all beautiful and interesting in their own ways. And their pictures are worth money, even though not so much as Jackie's.

Ethel is the warmest and friendliest of all the Kennedys, at least as far as a paparazzo is concerned. I first started taking pictures of her and Bobby during the 1968 election campaign. The fan magazines and the news magazines loved Bobby and Ethel. But it was even better than that. It must have been the Kennedy charisma. Bobby and Ethel attracted other stars to them. Stars like Liz Taylor and Richard Burton, Cary Grant, Andy Williams, Shirley MacLaine and Angie Dickinson almost became fans themselves for Ethel and Bobby. And ordinary magazine fans love to see pictures of all their stars together. I don't know why. Maybe it's because fans are lonely people and looking at a picture of all their stars together makes them feel like belonging to the group. And when the stars themselves become fans it makes being a fan respectable.

Right away I could see that even though Ethel wasn't as pretty as Jackie, she had a better personality, warm and

June 3, 1968: Ethel and Robert Kennedy at the Beverly
Hills Hotel. I covered Bobby's California campaign until
a few days before the assassination.

131

Bobby poses briefly with Ethel and Cary Grant at a $500-a-plate New York Democratic Party dinner. Below, Bobby attending the annual Bedford-Stuyvesant Benefit at the RCA skating rink.

friendly. It's always like that. The best-looking girls are stuck up. The girls who aren't so good-looking have to develop a friendly personality. Not that Ethel is homely. She has a nice figure and very lively and sympathetic eyes. She's very sensitive about her nose. I learned that the first time I was ever alone with Ethel.

It was in the elevator of the Ambassador Hotel in Los Angeles, where Bobby had his headquarters for the California primary. I was waiting on the landing of their floor for both of them to come out of their room, but Ethel came out alone.

"Where is the elevator?" she asked me.

"Right here," I said, and just at that moment the elevator showed up. She went inside and I followed her right in. She was very patient for the whole ride while I bounced my flash off the ceiling and took pictures of her.

"Just don't take my profile," she said, looking right at me and smiling. And I didn't. Just like with Jackie, I don't want to make Ethel look bad, I want to make her look beautiful.

And the pictures were beautiful. One of them ran on the cover of *Pageant*.

I had already left Los Angeles and was back in New York when Bobby was killed. It was a tragic thing for him to die like that, so near the "top of the mountain." I don't think there's any way to protect anyone in public from an assassin. No matter how good the security is, there's always a loophole. At that same hotel, the Ambassador, I once got into an elevator with Bobby alone. He didn't seem surprised at all that I could get that close to him with nobody else around. He just asked me who I worked for while I took pictures of him. And on another night I got into that same kitchen where Sirhan Sirhan killed him. If someone is really determined to get close to a person in public to take a picture—or to take a shot—there isn't much any bodyguard can do. The only thing I can suggest is stringent gun control laws.

I covered Bobby's funeral. At first, Bobby's press office at the Commodore Hotel in New York said I couldn't go to his funeral because I had applied late, and there was no more

At that same dinner, I took this photograph of Bobby and Jackie together. This was the first public event Jackie attended since the death of John F. Kennedy.

The fund-raising dinner attracted a number of celebrities, including most of the Kennedys.

room on the train. So I went home, gathered up all the pictures I had taken of Bobby and showed them to the people at the press office. Even Pierre Salinger was impressed. "Okay," they said, "You can go." And they found a seat for me on a chartered plane flight. My pictures are my credentials.

Of all the Kennedy women the one I admire the most is Rose. Rose has the strength to endure all these tragedies and still be beautiful, gracious and alert. She gets her strength from her belief in God, I would say. I was in Hyannisport once when they had a special requiem mass for Joe Kennedy, and after everyone else left Rose stayed in the church and prayed. I saw that I could get pictures without disturbing her so I took them. I don't feel badly about taking pictures of anyone in church. If I interfered with her that would be different. I believe invasion of privacy is relative to each individual. Some people are more sensitive than others. Therefore, I play it by ear.

After she finished praying, Rose came out and some tourists with box cameras stopped and asked her to pose. She did, and she answered all their questions including mine. I asked if Jackie and the children were expected in Hyannisport. She replied, "Just the children." Rose isn't snobbish. Actually, I think Jackie is the only one in the family who is snobbish. Then Rose got into her car and the chauffeur drove her off to the compound.

The compound at Hyannisport is the summertime headquarters for the Kennedy family, except for Jackie. Jackie sends the children to Hyannisport for the last few weeks of the summer, but she almost never goes herself. She doesn't seem close to the rest of the family.

Hyannisport is a small town, about a five- or six-hour drive from New York, just at the beginning of Cape Cod, a resort town where everybody walks around in bathing suits and with sand on their feet. There are usually two Barnstable policemen guarding the street to the Kennedy compound but I learned that they will let you through if you tell them you want to go to the church that's down that road past the compound.

One of the biggest assignments I ever had at the compound

Top, June 8, 1968, St. Patrick's Cathedral: I took these pictures at Bobby's funeral while Cardinal Cushing spoke. Lower photos were taken at Cardinal Cushing's funeral, Boston.

Again, the Kennedy family grieves.

At a special requiem mass for Joe Kennedy at Hyannisport, Rose stayed to pray after everyone else left. Afterward, she came out and talked with a group of tourists. Of all the Kennedy women, I admire her the most.

137

The compound at Hyannisport is the summertime headquarters for the Kennedy family, except for Jackie.

was to try to get a picture of Ethel together with Andy
Williams. There was a rumor that they were going to get
married and so I went up to Hyannisport to get some paparazzo shots of them. There's a rock jetty that juts out into
the water from the beach near the compound. I dressed like a
fisherman and staked out the beach from far out on the jetty.
I got some pictures of Teddy and Joan and some others, but
after a couple of days I found out that Andy wasn't there.

Okay, I told myself, if I can't get the pictures of Ethel and
Andy, at least I can get some other shots. If you don't get the
primary take, then try to get a good secondary take. I waited
for Ethel outside of church one day.

"Hi," I said when she came out.

"Oh," she said. "Hi." At that time she didn't know me by name, but she recognized me because she had seen me around Washington and other places.

"I have some pictures I took of you and Bobby," I said. "Can I bring them around to the compound?" That's a technique I use very well. I always ask if I can bring the pictures around later, instead of giving them now. That way I get a chance to see her again and get another take.

"Great," she said. "Bring them around."

When I got to the compound the guard took me to Ethel's lawn. She was sitting on the lawn in her bathing suit, but she was talking on the telephone with her back towards me so she didn't see me. The guard left me there and I waited. I could have taken pictures of Ethel like that, but I didn't. It was private domain. Would I have taken them if it had been Jackie instead of Ethel? I don't think so. The situation never would have come up because Jackie never would have let me get so close. You see, that's the difference. Ethel cooperates and Jackie doesn't.

Ethel fooled me. Not on purpose, I don't think so. But when she finished with her phone call she went right inside without ever turning around to look at me. But pretty soon some kids came out and I gave them the pictures along with a note, telling Ethel that I'd like to speak with her. In a little while Ethel herself came out. We shook hands and she told me how much she liked the pictures.

"I want to give you some money," she said, "because I know these are expensive."

"No. You don't owe me anything." I said. "I made money selling those."

"Oh," she said. She asked where and when some of the photos were taken.

You can really have a conversation with Ethel. It's nothing like talking to Jackie who never says anything more than a word or two.

"What I'd like," I said, "is some candid pictures of you and the children on the lawn."

"I couldn't do that," she said. "There are so many photographers who have asked for pictures. And I have to tell them no. It wouldn't be fair."

I paused.

"Do you know," I asked, "that I'm a paparazzo?"

"Yes," she said.

"Do you know what that means?"

"Yes," she said, "it means you don't ask."

"That's right," I said, and then I paused again. "Do you have any plans for the next couple of days?"

"Yes," she said. "This afternoon we're going sailing."

"Oh, good," I said. "I'll see you out there."

That afternoon when Ethel came down to the dock with

the children I was waiting for her in my bathing suit with my cameras.

"Oh," she said when she saw me, "I thought you meant you were going sailing."

That's funny. She must have thought I had my own schooner or something. I thought she might have been confused when I told her back at the compound that I would see her, but it wouldn't have been right for me to straighten her out. You never volunteer negative information. I stood there on the pier and got pictures of them getting ready and then I ran way out on the jetty when I saw them raising the sails. It was very windy out there and Ethel was having trouble steering and they kept bumping into another boat. But Ethel seemed to be having a good time. That's what I like about Ethel. She's a good sport.

And then there's Joan. Joan is the prettiest of all the Kennedys. I took pictures of Joan and Teddy in Hyannisport, but I think the best pictures I ever got of Joan was at a

I staked out the beach at Hyannisport to try to get a picture of Ethel and Andy Williams.

benefit at the Kennedy Center in Washington. I know that Joan said in *McCall's* magazine that she's shy and unsure of herself, but you sure wouldn't know it from the way she was acting at the party. This time she really seemed to be doing great. It was a terrific party, the best I've ever been to. Nobody even tried to throw me out.

Again my big assignment was to get a picture of Ethel and Andy Williams. And this time I did it. They were there together. I also told Ethel that it was me who shot the picture of her that was on the cover of *Pageant* that month.

"You must have retouched it," she said.

"No," I said. "I don't do any retouching." Maybe the magazine retouched it, I thought, but there was no need to tell her that. Let me repeat: Never volunteer negative information.

"Well," Ethel said with a smile, "keep up the good work."

I did. I got some good pictures of her and Andy. And even better, I got some great pictures of Joan and Peter Duchin. It

Ethel at Hyannisport. What I like about her is that she's a good sport.

Besides Ethel, I don't recognize any of these healthy-looking people.

was very spontaneous. Joan just decided that she wanted to play piano with Peter Duchin and so she sat down beside him. Now, most of the photographers who were standing right by the piano got shots of Joan and Peter Duchin. But I could see there was a better angle than that. And when you see the best angle, you've got to go after it, no matter what. Like anything else, photography is very competitive, and to sell your pictures you've got to give editors something extra, something no one else can give them.

In this case I could see that even though a shot of Joan and Peter would be good, an even better shot would be Teddy and Ethel watching Joan and Peter play. And to get that shot I had to put myself in the orchestra right in front of the trombone player.

When I told Ethel I'd see her out at the pier, she thought that I was going sailing too. She must have thought I had my own schooner or something.

142

"Haven't you had enough?" the trombone player kept saying, pushing the slide right by my ear.

There was one other special assignment I had to get in Hyannisport. And it was tricky because I had to paparazzo a teenage girl. The word was out that Bobby Kennedy, Jr. was dating a 16-year-old Hyannisport high school girl named Kim Kelly. The *National Enquirer* wanted her picture and they wanted it in a hurry. I took a morning flight on Executive Airlines up to Hyannisport, rented a car, and drove to the school. My number one mission was to get Kim Kelly, number two was to get her father, who worked as a bartender in the restaurant near the Airport, and number three, to get a picture of her mother.

The kids inside the school were helpful. They told me

I ran way out on the jetty when I saw them raising the sails. It was very windy and Ethel kept bumping into another boat; she seemed to be having a good time.

143

what Kim looked like and where to find her, but the teachers got very suspicious and wouldn't tell me anything. It's always that way. The lowest-level people are the most cooperative, especially kids. I left the school and waited for Kim across the street from her house. Pretty soon a Volkswagen drove up and a girl fitting Kim's description stepped out.

"Are you Kim Kelly?" I yelled out to her.

"Are you the guy who was looking for me at school?" she asked me.

"Yeah," I said. "I'm a photographer from New York and I have to get a picture of you." I showed her some pictures I had taken of Ethel and then I started taking pictures of her. But she was shy and kept turning away from me.

"You have to get permission," she said.

"We'll worry about that later," I said. "The main thing is to get the pictures." She didn't seem to have an answer for this.

Then a man came out of the house and started to call, "Kim, Kim!" That was her father and I ran after him to get his picture, too. Was I afraid that he might punch me in the nose? No, usually ordinary people don't do anything like

Ethel had a lot of trouble steering in that wind.

A family afternoon for Teddy and Joan.

Teddy at a benefit at the Kennedy Center. It was a terrific party, the best I've ever been to.

I finally got my picture of Ethel with Andy Williams.

that. Generally, they're flattered that you want to take their picture and if they don't want their picture taken, they just run away like Kim's father did.

Well I still had one hour before the last plane left for New York and so I decided to try for Kim's father at the place he worked. I went to the restaurant and asked for Kelly. They told me he was sick and wouldn't be in that day. But I was suspicious. I saw a guy who looked just like him duck behind the bar. First, I tried the direct approach and told him I wanted to take his picture. "No," he said, he didn't want any publicity. Then I tried to paparazzo him, but he kept ducking. Finally, I tried to outwit him. I pretended I had given up and was leaving, but instead I went around to the back and tried to sneak in through the kitchen. But he saw me again and he ducked into the freezer before I could get a good picture of him. He really got the best of me. And he was only an amateur. Beginner's luck, maybe.

If it hadn't been for my plane I could have outwitted him. After all, how long can a man stay in a freezer? However, my plane was leaving and I had to race to the runway where the plane was about to leave. On the way back I thought about Ethel and Rose and Joan and Kim and how friendly they were compared to Jackie. But with all her faults, there's only one Jackie. Yes, I was eager to get back to New York, back to Jackie.

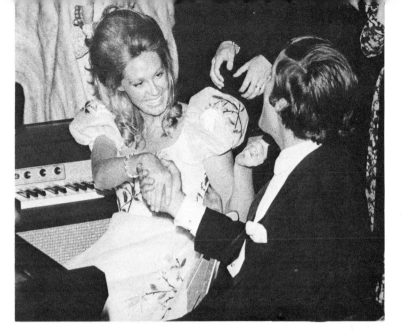

Meanwhile, Joan decided she wanted to play piano with Peter Duchin.

I had to stand right in front of the trombone player to get a picture of Teddy and Ethel watching Joan and Peter Duchin playing.

Joan says she's shy and unsure of herself, but at this party she was doing great—completely spontaneous.

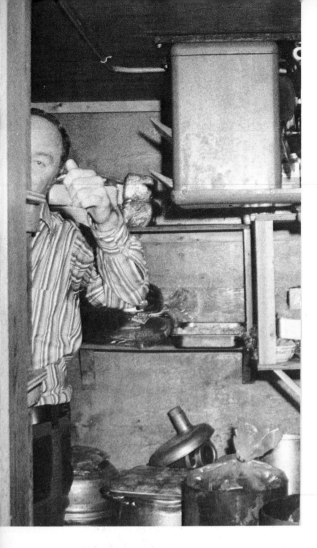

Bobby Kennedy, Jr.'s friend Kim Kelly was shy, but her father ducked me like a pro.

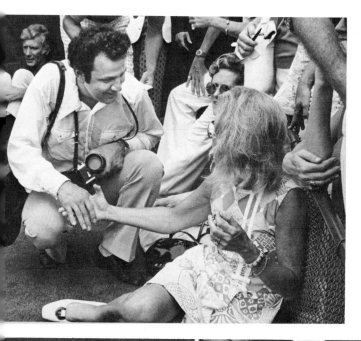

Ethel is the warmest and friendliest of all the Kennedys, at least as far as a paparazzo is concerned. She greeted me at the Robert F. Kennedy Memorial tennis match.

Teddy escorts his late brother Bobby's daughter, Kathleen, at her wedding.

9

"smash his camera!"

With Jackie there was always excitement. In the end it turned out to be too much excitement with lawyers, police, courts, injunctions and judgments. When I look back on it I ask myself: When did things really start going bad? I think it was that day in September, when I saw Jackie at the airport. It was the first day of fall. Maybe that was an omen. Summer was over and things were coming to an end. I have never seen Jackie as angry as she was that day.

It started like this. I hadn't seen Jackie in three months. I showed up at her apartment about five o'clock in the afternoon, just a spot check to see if anything was up. I could see right away that something was. A rented limousine was parked out in front, and that usually means action. And across the street John Martin was waiting. John's a guy of about thirty who works part-time as a travel agent but spends a lot of his free time watching celebrities. There are fans like John all over the world. About the only thing that's different about John is that he doesn't carry a little camera to take pictures and he doesn't get autographs. He just likes to watch the celebrities come and go and, since he reads a lot of fan magazines, he sometimes gives me good leads. When he does I give him $10. John got in my car and the two of us watched while Jackie got into the limousine.

As usual, Jackie put on her sunglasses as soon as she saw me, but what I didn't know was that this time she was really angry.

Jackie was furious.

Oh, I thought. I'll bet she's going to the airport to pick up Caroline and John coming in from Hyannisport. As I mentioned before, the children usually spend a couple of weeks at Hyannisport at the end of the summer. Sure enough, the limousine went over the Triborough Bridge and out to Kennedy Airport. Jackie went into the terminal to check out the arrivals and I went in after her. But I was keeping my distance, about 80 feet. As soon as she saw me, she put on her sunglasses, but there was nothing strange about that. She did that all the time. What I didn't know at the time was that she must have been saying to herself, "Oh, no! There's that same photographer. This time it's too much!"

I took two pictures and I turned to go outside the terminal to disappear for a little while. The big take I was really looking for was not just Jackie alone but Jackie meeting the children, and I didn't want to make myself too conspicuous before the children's plane arrived. But as I was walking away

154

When I returned, I saw her talking to agent James Kalafatis. I didn't have to be told they were talking about me.

She and Kalafatis wanted this police officer to lock me up—and from then on things went from bad to worse.

I heard this "clap, clap, clap" behind me like a woman's shoes hitting cement. I turned and I saw Jackie running right at me, her face red as a beet. She was furious. She didn't look good, and I never would have taken a picture of her like that, even if I had the chance. But I didn't have the chance because she grabbed me by the shoulder of my coat and she shouted to a passing policeman:

"Officer, arrest this man!"

This wasn't like Jackie, shouting and making a scene in public like that. I had never seen this before. I wasn't scared but I was shocked. I guess I was also lucky because the policeman was on his way somewhere else and didn't hear her. Jackie let me go and I went back to the car to tell John Martin what had happened. Then I had to make a decision. As I said, the real take I was after was the one of Jackie meeting the children. Was it smart to go back to the airport with Jackie in that kind of mood? Well, I finally decided to go back. Jackie is so changeable that I figured her mood had probably changed back to cool and composed.

So I went back. But I was wrong about her mood. She was still angry. As soon as I got to the door I could see Jackie talking to one of the agents, James Kalafatis, and then I could see them talking to a policeman. I didn't have to be told that they were talking about me. The policeman came over.

"Let's see your credentials," he said.

And so I pulled out my *Sydney Morning Herald* press card. The policeman looked at it and then at me.

"She's a VIP," he said, "Wait outside for her, not in here."

I did better than that. I left the airport completely, and John and I drove back to Jackie's apartment. I figured that I would forget about the airport reunion and get a take of Jackie and the children coming back to the apartment instead. I was waiting near the canopy when the limousine pulled up. But as soon as they saw me, Kalafatis and another agent, John Connelly, came right at me, pushing me out into the street. Before I knew it, I was right in the middle of 85th Street, trying to shoot pictures of Jackie over the cars and everything. The agents went too far that time. They shouldn't have used muscle. They knew that I was a member of the press and that I was no physical threat to them. They were keeping me away from Jackie and the children while they were letting a lot of strange pedestrians get close to

I drove back to Jackie's apartment and waited for the limousine near the canopy.

As soon as they saw me, Kalafatis and another agent, John Connelly, came right at me . . .

them. They knew who I was—yet they interfered with me and prevented me from taking pictures.

That was really just a preliminary to what happened next: the famous bicycle affair. It was three days later, September 24, 1969, and I showed up at the apartment in the late afternoon again. And again John Martin, the celebrity buff, was there. But this time I could see that he was worked up about something.

"They're in the park," he said, very excited, "on bicycles."

"What do you mean, 'they'?" I said.

"Jackie and John," he said.

I double-checked with the doorman, Pete Lee. Martin was right. So I went into action. I gave Martin the keys to my car and told him to get my other camera loaded with color film. In the meantime I set my motor-driven Nikon loaded with black and white film that I had with me at 1/500 of a second at 5.6 because I knew there wasn't going to be any time for adjustments once the action started.

I started up the path into the park. I didn't see them. Then, as I was walking down from the path, I looked back and I saw them coming. But from where they were they couldn't see me. I hopped over the guard-rail and crouched behind the bushes and waited for them, setting the motor drive for two or three frames a second and focusing on a bench about 40 feet away, using a 135mm lens to get the range of focus. When they whizzed by me, I got one of my

. . . pushing me clear out into the middle of 85th Street
. . . where I found myself trying to photograph Jackie through the traffic.

best takes. Now Jackie said later in court that I jumped out and frightened her and John and they almost fell off their bikes. But I didn't do that. I just stood there in the bushes and they never saw me. Nor were any of the agents around that time. So how could I have scared them? Actually, they were in the wrong. That was a pedestrian path they were on and they shouldn't have been riding their bikes. They broke a city ordinance and could have hit one of those old people. Hey, maybe I should have made a citizen's arrest! That would have been something. Later, in court, two agents submitted affidavits; one said I jumped out on the pedestrian path from the left side of the wall, the other said I jumped out from the right side of the wall at the end of the pedestrian path. Jackie said I jumped in the center of the path. At this time no agents were around at all.

Just as she reached the end of the path, Jackie must have heard my camera clicking and she turned around. That was the first time she noticed me.

"Oh. It's you again," she said.

But she still didn't seem terribly mad, certainly not as mad as she was at the airport. At least, if she *was* mad her voice wasn't showing it. Her voice was just cold and kind of matter-of-fact. I really wasn't ready for what was going to happen next. While Jackie and John waited for the light and looked for the agents, I took more pictures.

All of a sudden, I heard a noise behind me and I turned around and saw agent Connelly on a bicycle. He must have been trailing Jackie and John.

"You've had enough," said Connelly. He stood right in front of me with his arms up blocking my camera view like I was a quarterback and he was blocking my pass. I agreed with him. I'd had enough. I was even willing to forget about the color pictures and go home, even though John Martin had just found my color camera and was walking towards us. He is in the photos behind Jackie and John. I'd had enough. But not Jackie. That's when she said it, and I can still hear those words, loud and clear and angry:

"Mister Connelly," she said, "smash his camera!"

But Jackie's so clever. I really admire her for that. As mad as she was, while she was saying, "Smash his camera," she kept smiling. That was one time she really did have that Galella smile she was always talking about in court.

Connelly does his job without getting too carried away, too emotional. So I didn't really think he was going to smash my camera. Still, I'll admit I was nervous, and so I quickly picked up my equipment and started walking toward my car. In the meantime, I could see that Jackie had crossed Fifth Avenue and was half-way to Madison where she met and was talking with two other agents, Kalafatis and, of course, Walsh. Oh, oh, I thought, those guys do get emotional. Jackie

September 24, 1969: The famous bicycle affair. When I saw Jackie and John coming, I hopped over the guard rail . . .

. . . and crouched behind some bushes. I was about forty feet away when I got these takes. She didn't notice me until she got to the end of the path.

159

Jackie and John waited for the light to change and looked for a Secret Service agent.

I turned around and saw Agent Connelly behind me on a bicycle. "You've had enough," he said. I agreed—I'd had enough.

was gesturing towards me, and the next thing I saw was Kalafatis and Walsh coming toward me fast. My main thought was the film. I had to get to the car and lock my camera in the trunk before they could get it, and John Martin had the keys. I started to run.

"Stooooooooooooop!" Kalafatis yelled out, and that's when I really got scared. What happened if I didn't stop? Would the guns come out? I slowed down and let them catch up to me.

"Now you're going to get it," said Walsh, a little out of breath. "You're under arrest. I'm taking you in for resisting arrest."

"What arrest?" I asked.

"You'll see," said Walsh.

"There's no use going through with this," I said, "because I'm going to leave now anyhow. I'm covering a premiere."

In the meantime I was trying to edge up to my car and trying to get John Martin's eye so that he'd give me the keys.

"Give me the film," said Walsh, "and I'll let you go."

It's a funny thing, but the British Secret Service once tried to make the same deal with me. During the Ascot races I managed to sneak into the royal enclosure and I took some pictures of the Queen and her family. As soon as I did, the British Secret Service came right up and grabbed me. I didn't know that it was illegal.

"Give me the film," said one of the British Agents, "and then you may go."

"Well, okay," I said, "I'll have to take it out in a dark place."

So they let me go into a darkroom. They're gentlemen, those British agents. I took the film out of the camera, but I slipped it into my pocket and then I handed them a roll of unexposed film, making believe it was the roll they wanted. It worked. They took the unexposed roll and I walked off with the roll with the pictures of the Queen. But I didn't think the same trick would work with Walsh. He didn't trust me the way the British did. And so I had to try a different line. "No," I said. "It's probably no good anyhow. There was a lot of movement. It's probably ruined."

John Martin finally saw what I was trying to do and he gave me the keys.

"You know what you guys are?" I said, as I put the camera in the trunk and closed it. "You guys are sore losers. I'm going to fight this."

"Who are they going to believe in court," said Walsh, "you or me?"

Then Kalafatis drove up in the Secret Service car.

"Get in," Walsh said to me and then he looked at Martin. "You get in, too, to see what he gets."

And so the four of us drove over to the 19th Precinct on

67th between Lexington and Third. Walsh asked Martin what he did, and Martin told him that he was a travel agent. Other than that, there wasn't much conversation. The four of us didn't have much in common, except for Jackie, and it didn't seem a good idea to talk about her. Then we stopped in front of the 19th Precinct house and Walsh went inside. We had to wait in the car for ten, fifteen, twenty minutes.

"What's all this waiting?" I said to Kalafatis. "I've got a premiere to cover." I was pushing the premiere, but what I was really thinking about was that film. Back at my car the meter was running out. Suppose Walsh told the police to tow it away, and then somehow somebody would break into the back and take the film? What could I do about it?

"Officers, officers," I yelled out to two policemen in front of the precinct station. I managed to get one foot out of the car, but Kalafatis jumped out and pushed the door against me several times until I got back in.

"What's going on here?" one of the policemen said. Kalafatis took them a few feet away and showed them his credentials.

"If you're going to arrest me," I said, "arrest me. But let's get it over with. I've got a premiere to cover."

So they took me inside and arrested me. But it wasn't that easy for them. They really had to look hard for something to charge me with. Upstairs, in the detective bureau, I found Walsh and a city detective .thumbing through the books trying to find something to get me on. Walsh wanted to get me for assault, but the assault was on me, not Jackie or the Secret Service. Finally, Walsh got the police to book me for harassment, but not even for harassment of Jackie on the bicycle path. It was for harassment of Kalafatis in front of the police station! See, first they took me prisoner and then they found a crime to charge me with. Under the New York Penal Law, harassment is a criminal offense when with intent to harass, a person follows another in a public place, inflicts physical contact or engages in any annoying conduct without legitimate cause.

I took the summons with me, and John Martin and I went back to my car, relieved to find it was still there. Nobody had tried to break into it. Still, they never should have booked me on that phony harassment charge, and the judge thought so too. The case came up for trial before Judge Bernard Moldow of the New York City Criminal Court on October 23, 1969. Agents Kalafatis and Walsh testified and I never even had to take the witness stand. After the trial, the complaint was dismissed with a statement by the judge to the effect that "I'll say this, I am not certain who was being harassed; case dismissed."

Maybe it's too bad the whole thing didn't end right there. After that, things got worse and worse.

But not Jackie. Smiling, she said, "Mr. Connelly, smash his camera!" At that moment my friend John Martin (behind Jackie) was bringing me my other camera.

10

the fifty-yard penalty

Jackie, Jackie. Did it have to end like this?

Maybe so. I can see now that it was probably in the cards from the beginning. Both of us are strong-willed and determined to fight for our rights to the end. Jackie went too far in ordering the Secret Service to have me arrested. And the Secret Service was mistaken in listening to her. They never should have done it—brought me into court on that phony harassment charge. I had to hire a lawyer, Bennett Brown, to defend myself and he charged me $400.00 for his time and work. Why should I pay the bill? Jackie and the Secret Service should pay it. After all, I won. I requested the legal fee in a letter which my lawyer and I wrote to them. They never answered that letter.

After almost a year of head-on encounters and incidents, my lawyer, Mr. Brown, and I decided to take the next step—sue Jackie and the three secret service agents—Walsh, Kalafatis and Connelly—for malicious prosecution, false imprisonment, harassment and interfering in the pursuit of my lawful occupation. The complaint was served to Jackie on September 18, 1970. We sued for 1.3 million dollars in the New York State Supreme Court. Now I'll admit that's a lot of cash, and Jackie's lawyers tried to make it sound as though I was asking for 1.3 million dollars because Jackie wouldn't take her sunglasses off. But that wasn't it at all. Of course, I testified in court that I don't like it when she puts her sunglasses on. It detracts from the value of the picture. But I know she has the right to wear shades. I'm not complaining about that. What she doesn't have the right to do is to have the Secret Service continually interfere with my work, to bump me into the street, to harass me and to have me arrested. That's what I'm protesting about and that's what I sued for. The case was removed to the federal court on the

Jackie's apartment building from 100 yards.

U.S. Attorney's application because government agents were parties.

On July 2, 1971, the late Judge Edward McClean of the United States District Court for the Southern District of New York severed the three agents from the case on the basis that they were protecting John and Caroline. Therefore, they were performing their duties as government employees and were immune from suit. In their submitted affidavits, one of the agents claimed that I jumped out on the pedestrian path from the left side of the wall at the entrance of the path. Another agent said that I jumped out from the right side of the wall. Actually, when I took the bicycle take from the bushes, no agents were in sight. It was not until my complaint, as the plaintiff, against Jackie and the three Secret Service agents, based on the ground of their malicious prosecution, that

165

Jackie belatedly made a legal claim—the counter-claim—that *she* was being harassed by me, and used the bicycle incident as the galvanizing agent. She said that I leaped out of the shrubbery onto the center of the path causing John to swerve "violently" and frightening and endangering them. My six sequential photo-frames, Nos. 1-6, bear witness that they were taken unaware. Jackie contends that this was the end of the incident. My witness, John Martin, and I insist she later ordered an agent, John Connelly, to "smash his camera" (see photo-frames Nos. 7-15). Frame No. 15 was the last taken when Connelly stopped me. Then Jackie met and ordered agents John Walsh and James Kalafatis, who then chased after me, forced me and Martin into their car and proceeded to the police station. John Walsh, in his affidavit, states he was "checking out" my press credentials with the New York City Police when, in fact, he knew I was a professional photographer for more than one year. On one occasion, early in 1968, in front of Kenneth's Salon, I showed him some of my published work, such as "He Shoots the Stars," a profile on my work from Show Magazine which ran in the October, 1967 issue. I also showed him my press credentials long before that. It is a known fact that press cards are not necessary to practice free-lance photojournalism. The New York City Police Working Press Card is mandatory only when there are police or fire lines to cross. There were no such things on or around the pedestrian path on September 24, 1969, in fact. In the four years I have covered Jackie the only occasion where I recall a police line was at the Athens Airport and even then a police card was not necessary.

Alfred S. Julien, my principal trial lawyer, and an expert one at that, appropriately summed the situation up in court.

"What is this case about? It's about a photojournalist's right to pursue his occupation. That's what the basis of this case is. Does a man have a right to pursue his occupation as a photojournalist or may someone in high position, whoever he or she may be, whatsoever her position in our society, say, 'Where I am concerned you will take pictures when I want it [sic], and this area is carved out for me when I walk upon it, and that store is my private domain when I am in it, and you, photojournalist, I don't like your profession. I don't like you, and, therefore, when I am concerned you may not pursue your occupation vis-a-vis myself because when I walk in the street it is private. When I enter a public park it is private. When I go into a public museum this is private. When I enter a restaurant open to the public it becomes private!' "

To tell the truth, I never thought the fight would go to court at all. I thought Jackie would be reasonable and settle. In fact, when I saw Ari one night at La Côte Basque, well, outside La Côte Basque, he said to me, "I hear you're suing my wife."

Peace On Earth
GOOD WILL TOWARD MEN
☆
RON GALELLA
NEW YORK, N. Y.
☆
PAPARAZZO

This Christmas card which I sent to Ari didn't help my case.

"Yes," I said.

"Maybe we could settle this for a couple of thousand dollars," he said.

"Well, I'll have to talk to my lawyer," I replied.

"No," he said, "no lawyers. Lawyers bring publicity and I don't want publicity."

But I told him that I had to talk to counsel and I finally agreed to settle for $100,000. And so the next time I saw Ari outside the apartment, I told him my price.

"Oh, no," he said, "that's too much."

I told him that meant that we would have to go to court, which he said before he did not want to do. But I guess he changed his mind about publicity.

"Publicity," he philosophized, "is like rain. When you're soaking wet, what difference does a few drops more make."

Well, even if Ari wanted to settle, I doubted Jackie would. She didn't want to give me anything. She likes to win. She likes to dominate and she didn't want to be defeated by a paparazzo like me. I heard rumors at the time that one of her lawyers told her to pay me $7,500 to settle, and Jackie got so mad that she fired him. She didn't want to pay a cent.

Regrettably, I did some things that didn't help my case. I sent Ari a Christmas card showing me sitting on Santa's lap with Santa handing me a wad of money. There was a theatrical billboard next to us which said, "The Payoff" starring Aristotle Onassis as Santa and Ron Galella as the Paparazzo. I admit that card was in bad taste and I'm sorry I sent it. But it was nothing more than bad taste. Jackie opened that card and became furious, or she says she did. She wasn't even supposed to open it. I sent it to Ari, not to her. Anyhow, she said later in court that it was blackmail, that I was trying to blackmail her and Ari. Untrue. I sent out about 80 cards just like that one. It was my Christmas card for the year 1970. When you send out a blackmail note, you don't send out 80 copies of it to other people! Besides, it's sacrilegious to blackmail anyone through a Christmas card. I was raised as a good Catholic. Jackie did admit in court that she and her former lawyer, a Mr. McHugh, did not interpret the card as blackmail when she first received it.

Well, things got worse and worse. Everytime I turned around, there was some Secret Service man, or bodyguard holding his hands up in front of me like it was a football game and he was a referee. Yes, that's what it was like, a football game. I was always being stopped and pushed off the field onto the sidelines.

There was one very unlucky night when I spotted all of them, Jackie and Ari, Caroline and John, and even Ari's daughter, Christina, at the Metropolitan Opera in New York. I was looking forward to a wonderful evening—to a terrific take. Nobody had ever taken pictures of the whole family together. It would have been worth a lot. But I was blocked again and again. First, the Secret Service agents made a shield so that I couldn't take pictures of them in the Opera house. Next, they had me thrown out of the lobby and the public parking garage. Finally, they had a city policeman twist my flashgun, blocking my last opportunity. It should have been a rewarding night. But what did I get? Nothing. This was the most frustrating experience I ever had as a photographer. It could have been worth $10,000.

The worst was still to come: The Penalty. It started the same fall week I talked about in Chapter One, that same fall week that was probably the most successful week that I ever had. I think I know why Jackie ran away from me that day. She was protecting Caroline. She was like a mother deer and she knew that if she ran away, I would follow her and leave the fawn alone. That's okay. I don't blame her for that. She's a good mother and she was following her instincts. But, later at the trial, she used the same pictures of her running against me. She's so clever.

At the end of the week I got those pictures of Jackie walking on Madison Avenue and Joy Smith got those pictures of me getting those pictures of Jackie which appeared in *Life* magazine. My success must have been too much for Jackie. Her lawyers got Judge Cooper to sign a preliminary restraining order on October 8, 1971 which ordered me to cease harassing her. At the trial, she stated that I jump, alarm, startle, torment, touch her and the children, block their movements in public places, invade their immediate zone of privacy by means of physical movements, gestures or with photo equipment and place their lives and safety in jeopardy. She then got a temporary restraining order on December 2, 1971, which forbade me to go closer than 50 yards (more than a city block) to her or the children or closer than 100 yards (a football field in length) to the apartment. But Jackie outdid my suit. She asked for a permanent restraining order and for 6 million dollars in damages. Six million dollars from . . . me! At the beginning of the trial, Jackie dropped her claim for the bucks and asked only for the injunction.

I suspected right from my first day in court—February 16, 1972, in the United States District Court for the Southern District of New York—that I was going to have trouble. I was on one side with my three lawyers, Alfred S. Julien, Stuart Schlesinger and Bennett Brown. They were all intelligent men and they knew what they were doing. But on the other side, there was a lot of power. First, there was Jackie herself, the most famous woman in the world, the recipient of great sympathy. I don't blame people for being dazzled by Jackie. I am dazzled too. That's one reason why I took pictures of her. But that doesn't mean she's right all the time. With Jackie was a couple of billion dollars, courtesy of her husband Ari and the United States Government—that is, the Secret Service, and its counsel, from the United State's Attorney's Office.

They were all tough enough, but it was worse than that. Now I knew that any judge listening to the case was almost naturally going to be sympathetic to Jackie, the widow of a former president of the United States. But, the judge who heard the case was Irving Ben Cooper, who was appointed by the late President Kennedy. (Judge Cooper had a portrait of the late President in his chambers.) But worse than that, President Kennedy appointed Judge Cooper even though the Bar Association said it was a bad idea because Cooper was lacking in "judicial temperament." But even worse than that, Simon Rifkind, a former judge who had gone back to practicing law, who had appeared in Washington when Cooper had been nominated for the judgeship and supported that nomination, despite opposition, was now in the courtroom—representing Jackie! Oh, Oh, I thought; this could be trouble.

Before the trial commenced, I did sign an affidavit to have Judge Cooper removed from the case, questioning whether or not he could remain impartial in light of the fact that it concerned President Kennedy's widow and that she was now represented by Simon Rifkind. Later in its decision, the United States Court of Appeals stated that if I wanted to disqualify Judge Cooper, I should have made a formal motion to do so. The reason.why my attorney did not do so was that at a hearing before Judge Cooper on February 3, 1972, Judge Cooper made the following statement:

Compared to Jackie I was a nobody, yet under the American system I could have my day in court.

"Now, one last point and I think I am through. There has been placed before me a comment *which I could duck* because it has no pertinency to the merits of the application before us, *but I do not intend to duck it. I intend to meet it.* That is the point dealing with whether or not this judge should sit in this matter, and the inference is quite clear that the judge will prostitute his oath if he sat. I would not dignify so dirty an insinuation by any further comment with regard to it. Suffice it to say that *I here and now denounce the assertion,* and now for the remainder of all phases of this case, I overrule, in all respects, the objection to my sitting. Now, the plaintiff has a clearcut record that the objection has been interposed, the Court has ruled on it, and the fact that you reiterate it 50 times does not make it one bit stronger." (Transcript of Hearing, pp. 34-35, emphasis supplied).

The District Court ordered that testimony begin being taken in this case on the hearing for a preliminary injunction, contempt proceedings, and the trial on the merits, on February 16, 1972, which only allowed eight working days for my lawyers and I to prepare for a long and arduous trial, a trial which lasted from February 16 to March 23, 1972. Of those eight working days, more than half were tied up in taking depositions, 1-1/2 days on Jackie's which I was barred from, 6-1/2 days for my own. I did not have time to read these depositions at all.

The result of joining the contempt proceedings for violation of temporary restraining orders of October 8, 1971 and December 2, 1971, over my lawyers' objections, produced a lengthy trial of 26 days, a record of 4,714 pages, 25 witnesses and hundreds of exhibits. An examination of the record will show that approximately 3/4 of it was devoted to the contempt proceedings, instead of the focal point, which was the bicycle incident. My lawyers called upon only five key witnesses, the first of which was John Martin, to testify about the bicycle incident. Dudley Freeman, photo and news correspondent, now with the New York News Service, testified that I was very good at photographing celebrities in unrehearsed and unposed situations and those are the type of pictures that magazines requested. He also said that the public is interested in Jackie's comings and goings, what she wears, what she does and who she is with. Another witness we called was another free-lance photojournalist Tom Wargacki. Tom, a competitor of mine, testified that on several occasions the Secret Service agents did indeed interfere with my taking pictures of Jackie. Another witness we called was another freelance photojournalist, Lawrence Fried, who revealed his expertise of 22 years in the field, which includes publication in every major world-wide magazine and teaching and lecturing on photography and photojournalism. He is now President of the Society of Photographers in Communications, ASMP. Mr. Fried supported the proposition that my occupation of speculative freelance photojournalism or paparazzi is a recognized and accepted practice in the field. He testified that Jackie is the most famous lady in the world. He stated that it is necessary to get close to the subject, and the photographer cannot be restricted as to the distance to operate successfully as a photojournalist. "He also must be highly mobile, he moves a great deal, he stops, photographs, moves again, he is constantly fluid." He sometimes must follow a subject as long as a month to cover a story. My final witness was Mrs. Pat de Jager King, who is an editor in the pictorial magazine business and familiar with my work over a period of four and a half years. She testified that I was a recognized journalist, and a major source of photographs of Jackie, and that readers wanted to know about Jackie primarily.

Jackie's lawyers called a total of twenty witnesses, none of whom realized what a photojournalist has to go through to obtain saleable pictures. It has taken over twenty years of hard work and struggle to attain the expertise I have acquired in the field of photojournalism. Most of her witnesses were called for the purpose of destroying my credibility and that they did. There was Bernadette Carrozza, the former editor of *Photoplay.* Bernadette and I always got along very well. She bought a lot of my pictures. She even gave me a *Photoplay* press card for 1971 and 1972. I think Bernadette had a lot of talent for choosing good pictures and putting them together in an attractive way. By the way, when fan magazines like *Photoplay* buy my pictures, I have no control over the copy of the story. Many stars resent fantasy stories written about them. Mary Tyler Moore once said to me that she liked my pictures, but not the copy. But Bernadette really shocked me when she testified against me. I still don't know why she did it. Jackie's jet-setter friends Cheray and Peter Duchin testified. A photographer, Werner Kuhn, testified with pictures he took of the bicycle path that I was on the path when I took the photos of Jackie and John bicycling. He admitted he received $1100.00 for his services. There were a few more trivial witnesses like the assistant manager of "21" Club, who testified that Santa Claus stepped on his foot in front of the restaurant.

But even though I was nervous, I was excited too. This trial was a big event in the world of paparazzi, and I was there not just as a paparazzo, but as one of the stars. Most of the best paparazzi in New York were there, people like Tom Wargacki, Art Zelon, Brian Stein, Emily Barnes, Tony Camarano, Frank Teti and others. Frank is very determined, just like me. I'll give you an example. Frank lives in the "Little Italy" section of Manhattan, and when Paramount Pictures was filming one of the scenes from *The Godfather* on Mott Street, the scene where Marlon Brando gets shot, Frank stuck

172

March 7, 1974—at Richard Rodgers First Annual Dinner honoring Goddard Lieberson at the Pierre Hotel, N.Y. I approached Jackie's sister Lee and said, "Princess, we have something in common. We are both coming out with a book." She said, "Yes, and I'm writing it on my own." We chatted a bit and I helped her down the stairs. All the time she was smiling and friendly and didn't seem to mind being next to a paparazzo. I always found the Princess more cooperative and believe she likes publicity and shows it. She has her own individuality and has a serene beauty.

his camera out his window and took pictures. The studio got mad because they wanted to control the publicity. They wanted to use the public street to shoot their movie, but they wanted to keep all the publicity under their control. They told Frank to stop. This is what Frank told them: "You try to stop me and you know what I'll do? I'll play rock'n roll on my stereo very loud and ruin the sound track of your movie." That stopped *them*. I admire Frank for that. That's the kind of thing I would have done. And so I felt that when I was on trial, I wasn't standing up for just me. I was standing up for all paparazzi, for guys like Frank Teti. Also, this trial made legal history. Never before had a photographer and celebrity become involved over their rights. This case set a precedent.

Also, I was flattered by the fact that here I was with Jackie as an equal for a change. I was a nobody and yet under the American system, I could bring this great woman into court, where she had to defend herself, just like any other citizen. And you know, it was the first time, the only time that Jackie ever referred to me as "Mr. Galella."

During the cross-examination I noticed Jackie looking at her lawyers who appeared to me to be communicating with her as she was being questioned under oath. I caught them doing this several times. I told my lawyer, Al Julien, and he placed Bennett Brown, also one of my lawyers, in the jury box with the press to check this.

The New York Times called the trial the best off-Broadway show in town. Jackie made it a melodrama because she was the center of attraction. She said that she was a prisoner in her apartment, that she was terrified to go out because I was always there. You know, I looked it up in my records and I found that I took only twenty takes of Jackie or the children in 1971, my best year; only twenty out of 365 days! She said I was speaking disrespectfully, saying "Hi, baby," and "the Marines are back." I was called a voyeur because I went into Kenneth's salon without a camera to enquire whether Jackie was there. I didn't carry a camera because I didn't want to be recognized as a photographer. My camera was in my car which was parked in front of the salon. And then Jackie and her lawyers tried to make it sound like I was a sex fiend and a child molester, always jumping out of the bushes and grunting and bouncing all over the place to frighten them. That's stupid. Nobody could jump up and down like they said I did and take good pictures at the same time. And even if I could, I don't want to frighten them. The whole object of what I do is to make them look natural, as natural as they would look if no one was there. My photos reflect this and, therefore, they are my best witnesses. Magazines don't like pictures of Jackie and the children frightened by a photographer. They want beautiful pictures.

At the trial, Jackie denied that she was a celebrity . . .

And my pictures of them are beautiful. Even Jackie almost admitted that. All through the trial Jackie never complained that the pictures of her looked bad. She just took all the credit, that's all. She says she put on her "Galella smile" even though she was frightened. I don't mind giving her part of the credit. She is a beautiful subject. But I have to take part of the credit too. I am a first-rate photographer. With the modern cameras of today, it's not that difficult to make a good technical photo, so that things like the focus, exposure and lighting are almost always okay. But my pictures have more than that. They have heart, feeling and mood. And I think people recognize this. They recognize that I do capture Jackie just the way she is, with real emotions, not phony emotions.

I understand in a way why Jackie said the things she did on the stand. I do sympathize with her to some extent. There are places where photographers really do pester her, in Europe for example—the recent nude photos taken of Jackie by European paparazzi and published in *Playmen, Screw* and other publications. Everyone has a right to privacy, including Jackie, and I would never attempt such a thing. I can understand Jackie's dislike for the copy in a publication like *Screw*. She can't get at those photographers very easily, and so she gets at me, since I am visible. We were in court together for a month, and maybe now I understand her a little better, and maybe she understands me a little better. Anyhow, I'm not bitter about Jackie.

At the trial, Jackie denied she was a celebrity. She claimed that she· was just a housewife and mother—a private person. She denied that the public had any interest in her comings and goings, her apparel or who she was with. She showed a dislike of photographers, not just me. She said: "I am nearly always frightened by photographers."

The record shows that she is constantly being photographed by many photographers and has had conflicts with other photographers. For example, the 4 or 5 photographers who were pushed in front of a New York theater showing *I am Curious (Yellow);* the photographer who was arrested and fined $25 in Peapack, New Jersey; and the Greek photographer (Dimitri Koulouris) who supposedly interfered with the landing of one of Mr. Onassis' seaplanes and who received six months in jail for this.

Yet, Jackie and her lawyers tried to make the distinction that my behavior and conduct was different than other photographers, and that I, exclusively, caused her mental anguish. Yet, Jackie never complained that my pictures appearing in the press showed her in an unfavorable or embarrassing portrayal. She herself admitted in her deposition that my pictures never show her in an unfavorable light, nor do they embarrass her.

She accused me of flicking her with a camera strap, in front of her apartment, while walking to her limousine. On cross-examination, photographs were produced showing in

... **She denied that the public had any interest in her comings and goings.**

close sequence, since I used my motor-driven camera, that no such flicking incident occurred. The sequence shows a doorman was at all times between Jackie and myself, making any flicking or bumping a physical impossibility.

I am bitter about other people in the business who betrayed me, like Bernadette Carrozza. There's a lot of hypocrisy in journalism. There are some editors who buy my pictures, but who think I am a rat. They want it both ways. They want the pictures and they want to think that they are more ethical than I am and better than I am. Take Shana Alexander, for example. Shana Alexander is now a columnist for *Newsweek,* but she used to be editor-in-chief of *McCall's* magazine and a vice president of Norton Simon Communications, Inc. During the trial, she broadcasted an editorial on the CBS Radio/TV Network News one morning. Shana Alexander is supposed to be a good reporter, but she was very wrong this time. First of all, she said I made $100,000 a year off Jackie. That's nonsense. The best year I ever had was 1971, when I grossed $41,000; approximately half of that was from pictures of Jackie and her family. The rest came from selling pictures of other celebrities. The court subpoenaed these records. Then, she said I rent an apartment across the street from Jackie. Well, nobody rents an apartment across the street from Jackie because Central Park is across the street from Jackie. Shana Alexander ought to get out of her office and see where things are in New York. But I don't rent

an apartment anywhere near Jackie. My apartment, office and lab are twelve miles away in Yonkers.

Then, Shana Alexander called me a "piranha" because I make money off Jackie. Okay, I make money off Jackie. But I'm not the only one. While Shana Alexander was editor-in-chief of *McCall's*, the magazine requested pictures of Jackie and Ari from me to run on the cover and inside. They paid me, but I had to agree not to take credit for the pictures, because, I guess, I was too controversial for them. And other times, *McCall's* has run big excerpts from books about Jackie, books with some very nice gossip in them. So, if I'm a piranha fish, like Shana Alexander says, what are the people at *McCall's*—sharks? They made a lot more money out of Jackie than I ever did. But did you ever hear Shana Alexander criticize *McCall's?* No. It's okay to knock a paparazzo. After all, what can I do to her? But don't knock any of the big fish in publishing. You might hurt your pretty reputation in the business and find yourself blackballed some day.

Then there's the one person who burned me up more than anyone else, another paparazzo, Oscar Abolafia. Let me tell you about him and you can be the judge. Oscar is a paparazzo who has been hanging around town a long time. He has no formal training in photography. In fact, I had to show him how to do some things, like how to use a flashgun. Once, at Alice Tully Hall, he shot off many flashes in Jackie's face at close range (approximately 3-4 feet). Jackie was very angry. "You leave at once," she ordered him.

Oscar owed me a couple of favors. First, I showed him how to use the flash. But, even better than that, I introduced him to this pretty blonde Dutch girl whom he later married.

"I owe you a favor," said Oscar.

A big part of Jackie's case was based on one night in particular, the night that she went to see *Two Gentlemen of Verona*. Jackie complained that I had been pestering her all night and that I followed her and Michael Forrestal, her escort, and Peter and Cheray Duchin to a benefit at Bonwit Teller's before the theater and that just before the performance, I rushed down the aisle to take pictures and caused a big commotion. Peter Duchin testified that I was at Bonwit Teller's and at the theater before curtain time.

I wasn't at Bonwit Teller's. I had fallen asleep in a hotel lobby during the time they were there, and it was only by luck that I ran into Jackie at all later that night. I didn't rush down the aisle at any time. And Peter Duchin probably didn't even know who I was at the time. Stars almost never know one photographer from another. Joan Fontaine once said to me that we stars hardly notice who the photographer is, but we look into the camera they are pointing. And so how could Peter Duchin be so sure it was me?

The one person who could have cleared me was Oscar

Peter Cook and Dudley Moore accepted the New York Critics' award for Marlon Brando. Cook wasn't amused when I offered to autograph it.

Abolafia, because Oscar was at Bonwit Teller's, according to the Duchins, and he did rush down the aisle, and he did take pictures of her in her seat. I have seen his pictures. All he had to do was get up there on the stand and tell the truth. That's all I wanted him to do for me—get up on the stand and tell the truth.

But Oscar avoided me. Every other paparazzo in New York came to cover the trial, but not Oscar. Why? Because he didn't want to be subpoenaed, that's why. He didn't want to get up there on the stand and testify.

So my lawyer and I decided to have him subpoenaed. Now I know there is one way of catching up with any paparazzo. Just wait for a big premiere when all the paparazzi turn out to get pictures of the stars. And so, when *The Godfather* had its premiere on March 14, 1972, in New York, the process server and I waited outside the theater.

"There he is," I told the process server.

But Oscar saw us coming and he jumped inside the theater before we could get him and we weren't allowed to go in after him to serve him with the subpoena. He managed to sneak by us later when he came out. That's easy. It's no trick for any paparazzo to sneak out of a theater.

So there I was, betrayed by the guy who could have been my star witness. Later after the trial, Oscar admitted to me that he was in Jackie's lawyers' office twice.

In the meantime, all I could do was look at her. Day after day, I watched Jackie coming into the courtroom. During her days on the witness stand, the courtroom was jammed. As soon as she finished testifying most spectators left. Sometimes early in the morning before the session started I would stand at the window of my lawyer's office across the street and watch Jackie going into the courthouse with all the other photographers down there taking pictures. Of course, I was more than 100 yards away and so it was legal for me to take pictures. And I did once, to prove to my lawyer that it's impossible to get good pictures at that distance, and also to prove that she is a global celebrity which the crowds of pedestrians and press around her confirmed. But you can see that in New York you don't get much of a picture when you have to stand 100 or even 50 yards away, even when you are up high. Down in the street, when you have to stand 100 or 50 yards away, it's even worse because there is always some traffic or something between you and your subject. At night it would be impossible to get pictures because flashlight does not reach beyond twenty feet.

Looking back at the trial again, the Judge, Irving Ben Cooper, reprimanded me often—like he was swatting me with a fly-swatter, as if I was a pesty bug. Jackie's lawyers tried to get me to interpret "paparazzo" as a pesty bug. I explained that that was *Newsweek*'s interpretation of paparazzo

Judge Irving Ben Cooper, who presided at my trial, didn't seem disturbed by the paparazzi technique when I photographed him with Averell Harriman as he received the first annual Robert Kennedy Memorial award.

in an article they wrote on me. I testified that my interpretation is on my letterhead and business card which reads: "Photography with the Paparazzo approach." I defined the ideal quality of paparazzo photos as "exclusive, off-guard, unrehearsed, spontaneous, no appointments, the only game". My letterhead and business card were submitted in court as evidence of this.

During the trial, Jackie and her lawyers were trying to convince the judge that my behavior and manner of taking pictures was unprofessional. The judge even asked one of the agents to demonstrate in court just how I would take pictures. The agent held the camera inches away from someone representing Jackie and jumped up and down, sometimes as much as 11 inches off the floor.

One year after the trial, while I was preparing for a lecture, "Photography with the Paparazzi Approach," at Miami University at the 17th Annual Wilson Hicks International Conference on Visual Communications, I accidentally found among my contact sheets photos I had taken of Irving Ben Cooper before the trial, in 1969. These pictures show Judge Cooper getting the First Annual Robert F. Kennedy Memorial Award with Averell Harriman. Judge Cooper was only five feet away and he was smiling, not even aware that I was there. Too bad that I did not know that I had these photos during the trial. They may have demonstrated how I really photograph my subjects. You see, the reverse of what Joan Fontaine says is sometimes true: we photographers hardly know who the star or subject is that we are photographing.

The trial ended and I waited for the Judge to make his decision. I didn't think he was going to make any terrific decision in my favor, but even so I was surprised by how rough he was in his ruling. He said I would have to stay 50 yards away from Jackie, and 75 yards away from the children at all times. I was also to stay 100 yards away from her apartment and the children's schools. I was the only American citizen who was legally forbidden to walk on New York's Fifth Avenue between 84th and 86th Street for over 21 months; likewise with John's and Caroline's school streets. Like I say, with all the obstacles in the way, it would be impossible for me to get pictures of her, except maybe in the middle of the ocean.

Not only couldn't I take pictures of her at that time with that distance because I lost that trial, but she and her lawyers wanted me to pay her court costs which amounted to almost $20,000. The United States Government also wanted me to pay costs—$9,000; plus the Judge is holding me in contempt, for which he could fine me up to $10,000. Judge Cooper's judgment states that I am in contempt of court for violation of the temporary restraining orders of October 8, 1971 and December 2, 1971. He also holds me in contempt for failing to produce photographs in response to a subpoena connected with a pre-trial deposition. No written charge as to this was made until the entire trial had been completed. Then, without warning, Mrs. Onassis' lawyers started garnishing the editors that I deal with for their costs. I have put up all the court costs in the form of two bonds; they have continued the garnishments for over sixteen months. *The New York Times* reported that Jackie paid her lawyer $235,000 for representing her during the case against me, establishing the 25-foot limit on my photographing her. That figures out to about $10,000 a foot. Maybe I should become a paparazzi lawyer!

I was disappointed in the outcome of this trial. I thought America was the land of free enterprise. Now I have lost my innocence.

I think freedom of the press is an important thing. Therefore, I asked my lawyers to appeal Judge Cooper's decision in the United States Court of Appeals for the Second Circuit. The appeal was argued on April 10, 1973 before three Circuit Judges—Smith, Hayes and Timbers. It was decided on September 13, 1973. Two out of three judges decided that I was 87 percent right. Here's what they decided: The 50 yard injunction relief for Jackie was reduced to 25 feet and the 75 yard ruling for John and Caroline was reduced to 30 feet. The 100–yard and surveillance restrictions were totally dismissed. The transcript and court costs taxed against me have been reduced by approximately $4,000. I am gratified that the Court of Appeals has upheld my right as a press photographer to photograph celebrities. I will abide by the court's decision. However, I feel that a photojournalist or newsman should have a right to take pictures of any celebrity anytime in any public place without any distance restrictions. The court seem to regard this as a sport, like football—first they give me a 50-yard penalty, then a 25-foot penalty. I believe photojournalism is an art, not a sport, and requires freedom and control, like all other arts.

The United States Court of Appeals upheld Judge Cooper's negative interpretation of "paparazzo": "Literally, a kind of annoying insect, paparazzi make themselves as visible to the public and obnoxious to their photographic subjects as possible to aid in the advertisement and wide sale of their works." Then this footnote is added: "The newspapers report a recent incident in which one Marlon Brando, annoyed by Galella, punched Galella, breaking Galella's jaw and infecting Brando's hand." The court has failed to recognize my interpretation of paparazzi. As for the footnote on Brando, I feel the court should not have relied on newspaper stories in making its decision. The press does not always report facts accurately. This will give other celebrities license to physically attack newsmen and photojournalists in the future. Then what happens to freedom of the press?

I feel the court has not believed my greatest witness—my photographs—which were all subpoenaed into court and most of which are reproduced in this book. The greatest inherent quality of a photograph is its authenticity. It is believable. I believe they reflect no harassment or fright in their subjects. The Chinese have said for centuries that one picture is worth a thousand words, yet the court obviously didn't believe in this wisdom. Instead, they apparently believed Jackie and her lawyers' many thousand words.

The case started out with three Secret Servicemen pushing me around while I was taking pictures of Jackie smiling. When it ended, Jackie was still smiling, but not for me or at my camera, but at me. For although she started out as the defendant in my lawsuit, she managed to get a court order directing me to stay 25 feet away from her. No matter what happened, and although she is probably laughing at me, I am glad to see from recent news pictures that Jackie is still smiling. The ironic part is that she is smiling at my competitors' cameras, the ones who use the same paparazzo technique as I do. To use the court's phrase, "The paparazzo attack." You see, the paparazzi approach is the only true way we can inform the public about Jackie (and other celebrities).

She's so clever—that's Jackie for you.

Even though some snob journalists don't want to admit that I am one of them, how many of them have had their work in *Life, Time, Newsweek* and *The New York Times?* Most magazines and newspapers rely on freelance photographers. So I am a freelance journalist. Photojournalism is what I majored in; I have a degree in it from the Art Center College of Design. And if one celebrity can get an injunction to stop one journalist, why can't other celebrities do the same to other journalists?

It's going to be a tough fight, but we're going to win in the end. Celebrities cannot expect to be celebrities unless they accept and face the fact that when they are in public journalists and photojournalists alike have a right to inform the public about them.

11

the most glamorous woman in the world

America is infatuated and obsessed with youth, beauty and status. There are four kinds of wealth that make up glamour and the beautiful people. They are social, monetary, physical and psychological. Jackie has all four and that is why she is the most glamorous woman in the world. The social wealth she attained by marrying the charismatic John F. Kennedy when he was an up–and–coming politician with the Presidency in mind; the monetary wealth she attained by marrying Ari Onassis . . . his wealth has given her freedom and security to do as she pleases; and the physical beauty she inherited. A big-boned athletic body, yet graceful as a fashion model. She has large beautiful eyes, set far apart. She keeps her physical beauty by jogging, riding horses, which she loves, and through other sports, such as swimming and water skiing. In New York, Kenneth does her hair and Cyclax of London her facials. Last, but not least, the psychological wealth. Jackie has a quiet, intellectual, extraordinary, mysterious beauty. She is sensitive, poetic and independent. Perhaps when she discovers photographers or people looking at her, she almost always is on guard wondering, "What will they see or discover in me?", or, "What will they find out?" Jackie does guard her privacy. She is also artistic. She is a collector of antiques and 18th-century furniture.

184

It's over now between me and Jackie. Since the trial, I have not photographed her and when I accidentally see her, I avoid her. On one occasion, on January 10, 1974, Jackie, Lee Radziwill and Lee's two children attended the Liza Minnelli show. I got there during intermission and waited to see for the first time if I could take good pictures from the 25 feet handicap. I went into one of the boxes and focused on Jackie and her sister Lee. The range finder measured 28 feet, so it was legal, but it just was impossible to take good pictures because there were too many "gapers" in front of them blocking my view. This was my first test of the 25 foot penalty and I didn't take one frame.

But I'm not bitter. If I had to do it all over again, I wouldn't do it any differently, except I would have prepared myself better for the trial as Jackie and her lawyers did. Jackie and her expensive lawyers prepared well. Rather than attempt to answer *my* complaint that I had been arrested falsely, harassed, etc., they tried to show that I was a merciless, aggressive, leaping, grunting gorilla. (Agent Walsh spoke of me as Ron Gorilla in my lawyer's office once.) They also claimed that I had taken pictures of Jackie in spite of restraining orders by the court forbidding me to do so. Taking pictures of Jackie is no crime, whether she likes to have her pictures taken or not, yet that is what they have made it. I have no regrets. Of course, it's cost me a lot in time and money. Over 40,000 dollars in legal expenses, just about all I earned on her pictures.

I don't know if Jackie thinks about me anymore. Maybe

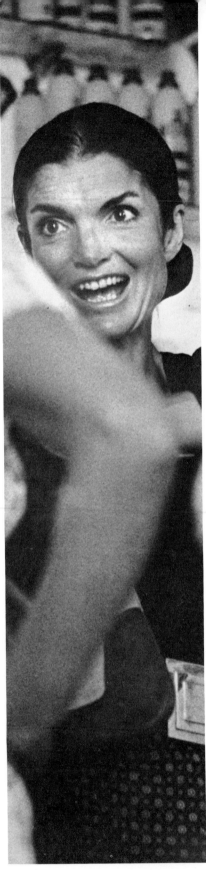

189

she does. Maybe everytime she goes out she still expects to find me there waiting for her. Does she miss me? Who knows. Is there anybody waiting for her now? I don't know.

I admit that I miss her a little. I think back to those years all the time. They were thrilling times. I remember wandering through Central Park on fall afternoons and all of a sudden finding her, like finding a diamond in the grass. I'll never forget *photographing* her in the streets of Capri or hiding myself in the coatrack in the restaurant in Chinatown. The challenge of trying to get Jackie and Santa Claus in the same picture—those were exciting times.

Even some of the bad times seem better now. At least I can laugh about a lot of them. The time I had to lie on the bottom of Zios' fishing boat going out to Skorpios and I almost choked to death on the exhaust fumes. Sitting in the car for hours and freezing to death waiting for Jackie and Ari to come out of "21" or La Côte Basque. When Agent Walsh and I had our showdown in Peapack. Even the trial, although it turned out bad, was interesting—one of the most exciting things that has ever happened to me.

What am I going to do now? Well, there are other stars to focus on . . . Liz Taylor, Elvis Presley, Ali MacGraw, Frank Sinatra. Maybe even Howard Hughes. Also, I think I'd like to get into paparazzo fashion, taking fashion pictures of models, but with a paparazzo approach so they look natural, not posed. I know that I'm always going to be a paparazzo. That's what I love. That's my way of creating, expressing myself. For me, photography with the paparazzo approach is the contemporary tool that captures the movement, the excitement in our modern world . . . where most of us are too busy to make appointments, especially celebrities.

Still, I know that no matter who I take pictures of now, no matter how beautiful the women are, there will never be anyone like Jackie.

What more can I say? Nothing. My story with Jackie ends like the one in *Cyrano de Bergerac.* Both are romantic trage-dies; both are filled with frustration, comedy and exaggera-tion. But my poetry is in my pictures and they symbolize Cyrano's white plume of freedom, my best testimony for posterity. So let me end it with pictures. Here are some of my favorites from over the years of the most glamorous woman in the world.

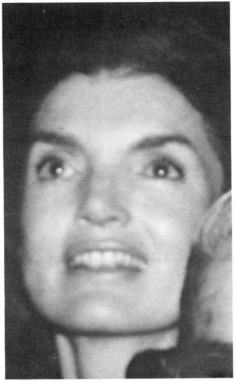

197

198

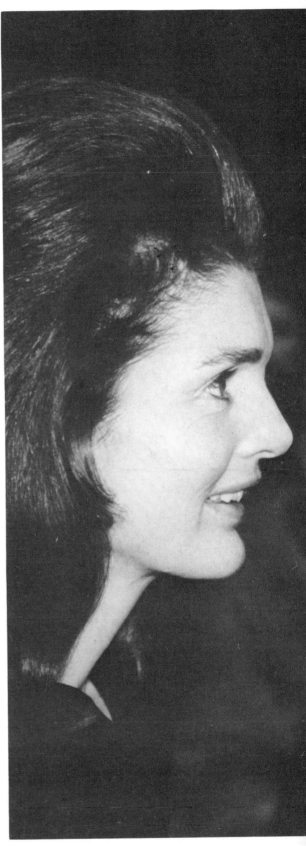

I don't photograph Jackie anymore. I leave that now to other paparazzi.